SUPER TV STARS

Richard Meyers

DRAKE PUBLISHERS INC. NEW YORK•LONDON

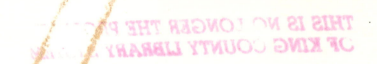
Published in 1977 by
Drake Publishers Inc.
801 Second Avenue
New York, N.Y. 10017

LC: 76-55091

ISBN: 0-8473-1509-6

Designed by Harold Franklin and Diane Fasano

Printed in the United States of America

CONTENTS

continued ▶

WORLDS FOR THE ASKING

This book is respectively dedicated to everyone responsible for it -- to the men, women, and others who are responsible for shaping people's minds and creating entertainment, to the seething mass that hurls alternate viewing on three major networks all at once out into the world. You've got the power when you're not floating in the void. Continue doing it good.

Thank you, *Fred Silverman,* without whom this book wouldn't exist;
Roger Corman, who's responsible for introducing and guiding young talent;
Brad Franklin, for doing what you could;
Dave Baltimore, for repetition, spaces, and bad backs;
Robert Vozza, short on brains but a snappy dancer;
Steve Schonberger, the Shalom Kid;
Jeff Rovin, for grit and long-distance telephone calls;
Craig Rogers, in advance;
Ward Damio, for disbelieving laughter;
Warren Murphy, for patient chagrin;
and, of course, thank you, *Melissa,* for the only reason there is.

SUPER TV STARS

The Happy Days Cast! From the left: Donny Most, Henry Winkler,
Grin Moran, Tom Bosley, Anson Williams, Marion Ross, and Ron Howard.

HAPPY DAYS

are here again (well, at least for the next two years)

Henry Winkler as The Fonz
Ron Howard as Richie Cunningham
Tom Bosley as Howard Cunningham
Marion Ross as Marion Cunningham
Erin Moran as Joanie Cunningham
Anson Williams as Potsie Webber
Donny Most as Ralph Malph

Nobody wanted to touch George Lucas in 1971. Because before that year George Lucas had taken his award-winning student short subject *THX-1138* and turned it into a full-blown Hollywood production with an all-star cast and the monetary contribution of a major motion-picture studio.

The studio bet that *THX* would be the surprise hit of the year. Science-fiction fans bet that *THX* would lead the studios into an era of intelligent science-fiction features. The filmmakers bet that *THX* would catapult them into notoriety.

They all lost. *THX-1138* bombed. Royally. Critics and audiences alike could not jive with the bleak futuristic tale of dehumanization. The film was panned, and the crowds stayed away in droves. The dream that the young George Lucas had of becoming a major movie force was shattered.

Well, not quite. George had another idea. An idea that led him to Roger Corman, the universally renowned king of the B picture. An idea that wound up in the production lap of Francis Ford Coppola, the man behind *The Godfather* and *The Conversation*.

Both Roger and Francis liked George's idea. They agreed to back and produce, respectively, a low-budget independent film. The idea was nebulously titled *American Graffiti*.

This movie, produced on a shoestring budget, using a then unknown cast, became the surprise hit of 1973. The story simply followed four boys—a sensitive middle-class youth, an intellectual joker, a class clown, and a cool delinquent—through their world of drive-in movies, hamburger joints, drag races, high-school dances, and hot rods in the summer of 1962. Sound familiar?

Around the same time in the cinema world Robert Mulligan and Alan J. Pakula were dissolving their partnership to pursue their own creative needs. They had previously teamed on a variety of films.

Pakula went on to direct *Klute, The Parallax View,* and *All the President's Men,* while Mulligan made *The Other* and a movie called *The Summer of '42,* which was about three boys—a sensitive middle-class youth, a boisterous jock, and a class clown—maturing into manhood on an island. Again, sound familiar?

Mulligan and Pakula are still looking for suitable follow-ups to their successes. By the time

FONZIE

Henry Winkler

Born: October 30, 1946

Place of Birth: New York City

Parents: Ilse and Harry Winkler

Nationality: German American

Educated: McBurney School for Boys
Emerson College
Yale School of Drama

Films: *The Lords of Flatbush* (with
Sylvester Stallone)
Crazy Joe (with Peter Boyle)
Katherine (with Sissy Spacek)

Height: 5' 6½"

Weight: 135 pounds

Eyes: Hazel

Hair: Brown

Hobbies: Pottery, plants, music, travel

Address: c/o Paramount Studios
5451 Marathon
Los Angeles, Cal. 90038
or
c/o *Happy Days* Production Office
Paramount Studios
Hollywood, Cal. 90028

you read this, Lucas has probably released his eight-million-dollar science-fiction extravaganza *Star Wars* in nine hundred theaters across the country.

In other words, this creative trio, completely different in looks, age, and temperament, has gone on to other things. But their synthesized contribution to cinema is still with us.

It took two more men by the names of Gary Marshall and Tom Miller to combine the themes of the two movies, *Graffiti* and *Summer,* or '42 and '62, and create a wildly successful television show.

Marshall and Miller took the fun-loving frivolity of *American Graffiti*'s mood as well as the sensitive middle-class youth, the joker, the class clown, and the cool delinquent; added a mother, father, and sister; changed the hamburger joints to Arnold's Drive-In; and, counting on riding the crest of the wave of nostalgia that was sweeping the country, created *Happy Days* for the A.B.C. television network in 1973.

Then they got the man who played the sensitive middle-class youth in the movie, Ron Howard, to play the sensitive middle-class youth in the show. Around him they gathered a top-notch, experienced crew of writers, directors, and actors.

Mike Rose and Harvey Miller were among the seasoned comedy screenwriters drafted. Jerry Paris, ex-actor and director of *The Dick Van Dyke Show, That Girl, The Odd Couple,* and many others, was to become their primary director. Marion Ross and Tom Bosley, who between them had a collective acting experience spanning more than thirty years, were signed. Ron Howard himself had been working professionally for almost twenty years. Even Erin Moran, cast as little Joanie, was a seasoned performer who had already appeared in three major movies.

And into this den of professionalism they threw a veritable beginner. Practically a novice. Even though he had been studying acting for almost a decade, he hardly had a professional credit to his name.

His name, by the way, was Henry Winkler.

If someone had told him on his first day on *The Happy Days* set that in less than three years he would be admired by millions, idolized by hundreds of thousands, and worshipped by countless others, the young Jewish actor would have probably run screaming from the studio.

The Fonz at his coolest. Ayyyy!

But nobody told him, so, unknowing, Henry Winkler put on his makeup, spent an hour getting his DA in place, slipped into his tight black boots, zipped up his leather jacket, and became—The Fonz.

CREATION

Henry Winkler was born on October 30, 1946 in New York, the son of Harry and Ilse Winkler. His parents were German Americans who had fled the Nazi horror of wholesale extermination in their original homeland. They felt themselves blessed to be in the United States and to be part of a wealthy lumber baron's family.

They sent Henry to the finest schools, first in Manhattan, then in Switzerland, in order to facilitate Harry's dream, that his son would become a diplomat. Or at least a part of his international lumber business.

But, as Henry later said, "If you're born to be an actor, that's what you do."

His parents and peers didn't see it that way. His sophisticated relatives tried to pry him from his goal with cultured disdain. They said that the acting profession was too hard, too insecure, and too nebulous. No person of "quality" was in "that business." His associates couldn't believe that a boy who had everything—breeding, opportunity, wealth—would gamble it all for a theatrical career.

But Henry was a dreamer. He dreamed of becoming an actor. And, because of all the pressure on him to do "the right thing," he became a loner. He did the minimum that was expected of him, but he still didn't fit in; his grades dropped and his yearning for an acting career grew. Little by little he began to discover that "the right thing" was wrong for him.

When he was young, it seemed to him that the only way to be popular was to be athletic or good-looking. But, in Henry's own estimation: "I was not what you might call the handsomest kid on the block. Dustin Hoffman hadn't come along yet to make short guys with dark hair and prominent features sex symbols.

"I figured that since I'd never have [popularity], I might as well spend my time and energy running after things besides [it]."

Henry graduated and went to Emerson College in Boston, a school in which scholastic achievement is played down and individual growth is stressed. If you wanted to study psychology while appearing in dozens of plays a year, you could at Emerson. And that's just what Henry did. (I know of which I speak: I, the author, spent two enjoyable years at Emerson doing cartoons, making films, appearing on college-TV productions, as well as acting in eight plays, playing eleven roles!)

Henry began to experience a new form of self-expression. Rather than making a reputation or playing the "game of obligation," as so many young people do, he found that he could communicate his inner feelings by living out his dreams through the creation of a totally new character.

Henry Winkler discovered acting. In acting he found that "[people] both with whom you act and those who see you act respond to you differently."

His new-found passion, once a childhood fantasy, had become a plausible reality. After Emerson, on the strength of his enthusiasm and the skill of his audition, Henry was accepted into the Yale School of Drama, one of the best theater schools in the country. (The other two, by popular and scholastic measure, are Boston University and Carnegie-Mellon.)

Once entrenched in New Haven, Connecticut, Henry became involved with the college's repertory theater, and his talent secured him not only more than sixty roles in the next five years but also parts in New York commercials for products ranging from toothpaste to pizza.

It wasn't all cake and cream, though. Henry was still having difficulty in relating to other people. Acting is an insecure art, after all, and, in order to be a good actor, one must, like Henry, be sensitive. And sensitivity can cost you in the big, bad world.

So, on the one hand, Henry was secure and successful at the Yale Rep, while, on the other hand, he wanted to grow both as an individual and as an actor.

"I have to prove myself as an actor," he says. "I have to learn to expand as a person so that I can enjoy and contribute to a strong personal relationship."

Henry left Connecticut when a better-paying acting job was offered to him. He moved to another theater in Washington, D.C., hoping for

The original Fonzie, cloth jacket and all, giving Richie Cunningham some first season counseling.

more success and a wealth of new experiences. He was fired less than a month later.

Thankfully, he has a double edge to his sensitivity. Its foundation is strength. As he put it: "If you don't take the chances, you don't grow. You wither."

CATHARSIS

Around that time some men who specialized in commercials wanted to break into the movie biz. But they did not have the money or the studio clout to make the break big. So they worked up what they felt was an eminently sellable idea called *The Lords of Flatbush* and sent out a casting call.

Their movie was another growing-up-in-the-fifties film but from the point of view of a couple of streetwise toughs in Flatbush, New York. Out of the final cast you can pick the names of Perry King, Sylvester Stallone, and Henry Winkler. Henry played the supporting role of Butchey Weinstein, a tough, tight-panted, ducktailed, rough-talking high-school hood.

Winkler had only to remember his own youth to bring his characterization of Butchey into perspective. Henry remembers: "When I was growing up in New York, I was scared to death of guys like him. If I saw him coming down the street, I'd walk two blocks out of the way."

Unfortunately, he had very little opportunity in *Lords* to display his developing acting talent. All the heavy drama was delegated to King and Stallone. Perry played a thug who was trying to love someone out of his league, a punk having an affair with a prom-queen type, while Sylvester played a cuckolded hood who was led by his nose to the matrimonial altar by a shrewish teenage girlfriend.

The movie, when it was released in 1974, was viewed as a cheap, harmless oddity. It was a relative success with the drive-in crowd, the kind of people that the movie portrayed, but critically— reviews being so important to a young actor's continuing success—it went nowhere.

Even when it was reviewed—for example, in *Time Magazine*—Winkler's contribution was glossed over, mentioned only in parentheses: "Butchey Weinstein (Henry Winkler) just sort of hangs out and waits for the future to pass by."

The film quietly disappeared, but, contrary to what the review said, Henry didn't wait for the future to pass by. Neither did the rest of his fellow cast. Perry King went on to star in *The Possession Of Joel Delaney* with Shirley MacLaine, *Mandingo* with Ken Norton, *The Wild Party* with Raquel Welch, and *Andy Warhol's Bad*. Sylvester Stallone, meanwhile, couldn't find work, so he wrote and starred in a little number called *Rocky* (but that's another story).

But back to our hero. Henry Winkler worked at the New York Showcase Theater and secured another hood role in *Crazy Joe* with Peter Boyle. But even while Henry was reexamining his career, a concept was taking shape all the way across the country.

Mike Eisner of A.B.C. and Tom Miller of Paramount had thought up the initial idea for *Happy Days* as far back as 1970. The more the two talked about giving the public a charming slice of life fifties style, the better the idea sounded. Soon Eisner was so enthusiastic that he commissioned Miller to go ahead and write a pilot.

Miller brought in the experienced Gary Marshall to do even better than that. He swept Marshall into the spirit of the thing, and Gary soon produced a short film about a middle-class family in the fifties.

Meanwhile, back at the network (as they say), the powers that be frowned on the entire idea. They thought that nobody was interested in that era of history. But, educated in the ways of the dollar, they did not let the Gary Marshall short subject go to waste.

Some night, if your local TV station televises reruns of *Love, American Style* and you see a segment about a family called the Cunninghams and their first TV set, watch carefully. You will be seeing the original pilot of *Happy Days*.

A year after the exile of the Miller-Eisner-Marshall idea George Lucas met Roger Corman and Francis Ford Coppola, and audiences all over the world flocked to see the adventures of four boys in the fifties. *American Graffiti* was making money hand over foot.

The A.B.C. brass suddenly thought that a fifties TV show might be just that ticket. While they congratulated themselves, Eisner did something about it. He told Miller to tell Marshall to begin filming the concept of *Happy Days*.

But Marshall had had time to move back a bit

A little flying "Ayyy!" service from the Fonz in the garage for Ralph.

and critically survey his work. When faced with the order to film one of the three backup scripts that he had prepared during the previous filming, Marshall balked.

He told Miller that the show needed something. It needed something to make it tougher, meatier, stronger.

"We need the street element," he said, "and it can be done by adding just one character."

When Miller asked who this character was, Marshall told him about a kid whom he had known when he belonged to a New York street gang called the Bronx Falcons. Marshall would base a *Happy Days* cast member on this incredibly cool kid.

Miller asked him what the character's name would be. Marshall told him. Arthur Fonzarelli.

No one could have convinced them then of the impact that their character would have. They would never have believed it. If they could just have looked a few years in the future . . .

Henry Winkler had gotten himself an agent. A person couldn't get commercial and movie roles by himself anymore. The acting profession had become a dog-eat-dog proposition in which an estimated thirty thousand acting students a year graduate into a reality of way too few parts available.

But Henry was talented and had matured into a formidable presence. Intense, full of energy, he maintained a control of his skill that was perceivable only when he was acting. Even when the less-trained eye dwelled on him, his wiry frame, sandy brown hair, and sharp features demanded attention.

Henry's agent knew that he was good, and, for a good actor, he knew where the action was. California. Hollywood. His agent urged Henry to go to Los Angeles.

But Henry liked the East Coast. He was doing well there and was afraid that going out to Tinseltown would make him just another face in the crowd.

Henry will admit that fear affects him, but he will also admit: "Fear isn't necessarily bad. It can be very healthy, very motivating. It is an individual's responsibility to take his own fear and make it work for him. Having fear is not what's crucial. Knowing how to deal with it, how to relate to it, is what's important."

Soon Henry knew what to do with his fear. He faced it and followed it into the lion's den. He made the move to California. So, while Marshall and Miller were collecting their cast and crew for *Happy Days* and trying to find just the "right" guy for the role of Arthur Fonzarelli, Henry Winkler was appearing on the TV show *Rhoda*.

I, the author, was watching television one day two years ago, just after leaving my own theatrical career to pursue a dubious literary road. Dubious because I had just spent twelve years in the theater. Dubious because my editor may think I stink. Dubious because I felt that only after twelve years did I really know what it meant to act. To fully conceive the work and the control needed to create a total character. Even after leaving the stage I delighted in seeing the seemingly effortless combination of technique and style.

I was always expansively pleased with any actor who could make me forget that he was acting. I was delighted by the ability of a Robert De Niro or a Roy Scheider.

On that day two years ago I was downright amazed by a young actor on that early segment of *Rhoda*. The man was playing a lecherous real-estate agent and had, I swear, no more than seven lines. But in that short time he so fully realized his role that I was floored. I waited through the closing commercials to get the actor's name. It was Henry Winkler.

I had, of course, heard of *Happy Days*, but I thought it was just another nostalgia show. The network's way of trying to placate the seething seventies masses by creating a falsely idealized view of the fifties. I caught up with the show just before The Fonz caught up with the public.

Henry Winkler caught up with Gary Marshall and Tom Miller about two months after taping the *Rhoda* episode that so stunned me.

The producers had visualized an actor with the physical presence to match the mental picture they had of Fonzie. In other words, someone at least seven feet tall. So, when the five-foot, six-and-one-half-inch Winkler walked into their offices, the story goes that Miller could hardly contain his surprise.

Henry had reportedly argued with his agent about showing up for the Fonzarelli auditions in

Henry Winkler as Arthur Fonzarelli.

the first place, and Miller's reaction only reinforced Winkler's preconception of doom.

"I'm not what you're looking for," said Henry incredibly. "I don't want to waste your time."

It's hard to believe that an actor with Henry's skill could be so insecure. Miller said later that Henry was "unassuming and polite, with impeccable manners and openly nervous."

Cindy Willians, TV's Shirley of *Laverne and*, says it more succinctly: "[Henry is] analytically intense and polite to the point that you want to tell him, 'knock it off.' "

But back to our story. Intrigued by Henry's reticence, Miller got him to study a few pages of script. Then, as Miller tells it: "He turned his back for a second, and, when he turned around again, I'd never seen such a total transformation in my life. In that one second he became Fonzie and actually seemed to have grown a full foot in height."

According to another source Miller was even more effusive: "He turned his back on us for five seconds, and, when he turned around again, suddenly he was ten feet tall."

A difference of nine feet. It was all the difference between the first season and the third.

CONTINUATION

The rest of Henry's march to the small screen was icing on the cake. The A.B.C. brass were as impressed with him as the *Happy Days* producers were. Suddenly there was a contract, a cast, a crew, and the Cunninghams.

Unfortunately, there were no Fonzie characteristics. Fonzie was only a name. Marshall had considered his power and presence but had not etched him into the *Happy Days* landscape as he had the rest of the characters.

The initial stories concentrated on the trials and tribulations of your average American family during the fifties in Anytown, U.S.A. The Fonz was delegated to the billing and screen time of, say, Ralph Malph.

And why not? The Fonz and Henry were unknown variables at that time. Rightfully, the weight of the show belonged on the shoulders of the old pros, Ron Howard and Tom Bosley.

Ron Howard is twenty-three years old. Ron Howard was born March 1, 1954. Ron Howard made his professional stage debut with his parents at the age of two. Ron Howard made his professional screen debut with his father and Yul Brynner at the age of four (the movie was *The Journey*, which was apt, since Ron had to travel all the way to Vienna, Austria to make the film). Ron Howard was a seasoned pro by the time he was six.

In 1960 he starred on *The Andy Griffith Show* as Opie. While he was making two hundred forty-nine episodes he spent his "free" time by appearing in:

(1) *Five Minutes to Live*, a 1961 potboiler starring Johnny Cash (yes, *the* Johnny Cash) about fugitives, country singers, murder, extortion, rape, and small-time life;

(2) *The Music Man*—Ron had the leading child role of Winthrop Paroo opposite Robert Preston's Harold Hill and Shirley Jone's Marion the librarian;

(3) *The Courtship of Eddie's Father* with Glenn Ford—the *New York Times* called Ron "frighteningly precocious."

Besides filmwork and duties on the Griffith show Ron visited *The Red Skelton Show*, *Dobie Gillis*, *The Twilight Zone*, *Gunsmoke*, and *The F.B.I.* in a guest-star capacity.

In 1968 at the age of fourteen Andy Griffith's show was cancelled. One might think that the young man had had enough of the wear and tear of television. Not Ron Howard.

As he put it: "The important thing was that I was a child actor. Not a child star. There's a world of difference."

Indeed there is. Ron went to work right away with Henry Fonda on the ill-fated TV situation comedy *The Smith Family*. After a year it was cancelled, but Ron didn't lack for work. He starred in TV movies and guest-starred on other shows. Not only was Ron blessed with endless youth but also with a natural ability and a professional demeanor as well.

"Whatever I am, I can thank my mom and dad," he says, "Both of them were actors. So they knew what it was all about."

Not only that, but they didn't force the limelight on their son as many misguided parents do in trying to live out their failed glory through their children. Mr. and Mrs. Howard gave Ron the opportunity to perform, saying that, if he didn't like it, he wouldn't have to do it.

Ron Howard and Cindy Williams meet American Grafitti's version of the Fonz, Paul LeMat.

But Ron loved it. He found that keeping up with pros made him feel good. And he kept up with the best of them. Almost effortlessly, Ron seemed to prove himself by not trying to prove himself. Not only did he hold his own with the likes of Fonda, Ford, Griffith, and Jimmy Stewart, but he stood up alone in the spotlight for *American Graffiti*.

Almost ten years had passed since his last recorded film role. That of Genius in the B film *Village of the Giants*. There was quite a difference between the sensitive middle-class youth whom he was about to play and Genius. Genius, in the picture, had invented a substance that, when eaten, created giants. Then, in time for the finale, he invented a gas that shrank giants. (As a footnote to a history of the cinema, *Village of the Giants* was the one and only film to be presented in "perceptovision," whatever that was.)

So it was quite a jump for him to be starring in the sleeper smash of '73, *American Graffiti*. A jump but no real surprise (his costar playing the role of his high-school sweetheart, was Cindy Williams, but more about that later). It is impossible not to assume that the fact that Ron was cast as Richie Cunningham in *Happy Days* was a direct result of his fine showing in *Graffiti*.

Tom Bosley seemed to appear fully blown (if you'll excuse the expression) as Howard Cunningham, Richie's father and Fonzie's foil on *Happy Days*. But what many people don't know is that his distinguished career on stage and in films spans almost thirty years.

His experience and talent are in abundant evidence every week on the show. Among the many credits of which he can boast are:

(1) The leading role in the Pulitzer Prize-winning Broadway musical *Fiorello*. The *New York Times* said of him that Fiorello was "extremely well played by Tom Bosley, who is short and a trifle portly, has a kindly face, abundant energy, and an explosive personality."

(2) Film credits in movies with Steve McQueen, Peter Sellers, Dick Van Dyke, Jason Robards, Paul Newman, Lucille Ball, Henry Fonda, and Natalie Wood, playing roles as diversified as a shy shopowner, an eccentric inventor of a gun-slinging robot, and a general in World War II who is caught by the Nazis in a Tunisian Turkish bath.

(3) Just before he was cast as Howard Cunningham, he did a magnificent job as a bum who is willing to give up his eyes for cash in the pilot of Rod Serling's *Night Gallery*, directed by Steven Spielberg, who went on to helm *Jaws* and *Close Encounters of the Third Kind*.

As the *New York Times* says about the 1968 stage production of *The Education of H*Y*M*A*N K*A*P*L*A*N*, "Whether singing, dancing, or just plain acting, Tom Bosley was constantly admirable."

In everything, Mr. Bosley, I agree.

Happy Days appeared on the schedule in January 1974, four months before *The Lords of Flatbush* would be released. The show continued through the remaining thirteen weeks of the season true to its original form. Entertaining but lightweight tales of teenage frustration unfolded to a moderately large audience.

The basic framework of the first season was: "Richie tries something on the urging of Potsie. Richie gets embarrassed." Or: "Richie tries something on his own. Richie gets embarassed." Or: "Richie does something with his family. Richie gets embarrassed."

At first, watching the show caused emotions very near to agitation. Everything humorous seemed to lead up to or build Richie's discomfort. "Such is the lot of growing up," the show seemed to be saying. Even though the mild-tempered Howard would always be there to lend support, all I remembered of the first season was each of Richie's defeats.

Everything about the show seemed to lend itself to that theme. The Cunningham's living room was small and closed-in. The show was on film and dark, with a laugh track. Originally, the character of Potsie Webber, played by Anson Williams, was based heavily on Oskie, the character in *Summer of '42*, a gregarious, cocksure jock with only one thing on his mind. That is, a three-letter word beginning with "s," ending with "x," and having a very popular vowel in the middle.

The mood of the show was also heavily borrowed from both nostalgic movies ('62 and '42). The creators well knew that humiliation could be funny. Woody Allen was prospering as the main bastion of that kind of humor. (Mikey Rose, one of the show's writers, cowrote several of Allen's films, including *Bananas* and *Sleeper*.)

The show that started it all. The legendary last show of the second season. The Fonz's first television love.

So, while Richie and his friends were painfully maturing in front of millions, Henry Winkler was developing The Fonz. Fonzie, during that first season, remained a nebulous force. A mystery. A head in the next booth in Arnold's that would turn and deliver his opinion in an expression or a hand signal instead of a word.

Even then Arthur Fonzarelli was largely a Winkler creation. The thumbs-up sign was his. The leather jacket and boots were his (literally—he took them from his role as Butchey Weinstein in *Lords*). The script and wardrobe people supposedly wanted The Fonz to wear a cloth jacket and penny loafers. The cloth jacket he wore for awhile—you can see it in the reruns. But penny loafers? Winkler drew the line.

Henry was basically free to create. After all, he didn't log much screen time, and what there was of that presented an enigmatic view of The Fonz. What was he? A hood? An incredibly successful makeout artist? All we, the audience, knew about him was what was whispered in awed tones by Richie and his friends.

The final thing in Henry's favor was that he honestly wanted what was best for his character and for the show. The rest of the cast looked with respect at his honest integrity and conceptual thinking. Taking a surprisingly cerebral acting approach given the character, Henry fleshed out The Fonz.

"I believe an actor, a good actor, adds something to what is already laid down," said Henry at one point. "And that certain addition, that unique something, is what makes him or her an artist and the role played a memorable one."

Henry brought his unique something to his role. He gave to the physical Fonz, a seemingly short, sharp-featured man, an assurance worthy of a mental giant. He added the pauses, the turns of a phrase, the "ayyyyy."

But then, instead of leaving the character's development to its natural course as dictated by the script, Henry gave The Fonz a purpose, a direction. He saw Fonzie as a guy who was desperately trying to fit in but afraid that he might be rejected.

That was the "certain addition" that did the trick. That was what Henry added. On the surface Henry and Fonzie were as different as angel food cake and lasagna, but underneath, where it counted, they were brothers. Both wanted to fit

in, but, afraid, Henry became an actor; The Fonz became supercool.

Fonzie was still mysterious, still powerful. But now he was not only that but also watchable, vulnerable, and, most importantly, lovable.

And just in time, too. For the public seemed to grow tired of watching losers in *Happy Days'* second season. The pedantic failures of Richie, the homespun humor of the Cunninghams, and the nostalgia weren't enough. The ratings began to slide.

Happy Days was in the bottom twenties when Tom Miller and Gary Marshall made a monumental move and took a tremendous gamble. Since they had nothing to lose, they pulled out a bottom card, put it on top, and reshuffled the deck. In other words, they pulled Fonzie out of the background, dusted off his leather, and put him on center stage in the spotlight.

They had slowly been strengthening Richie's character and mentally weakening Potsie's, so now they pulled out all the stops. Richie was made not just intelligent but downright wise at times. Potsie was corroded until he was a putz, the brunt of most of the humiliation once reserved for Richie. And Ralph was wisely developed into a stopgap, a usable character who could fit into many different scenes at the drop of a joke.

Knowing how important audience reaction was to their actors (not to mention to the network), Marshall also brought in a live audience and switched to videotape. The Cunningham's living-room set was opened up and lightened. Most of the cast were ensemble actors, so ensemble work was stressed.

The first segment to be taped in that way was the last show of the second season. In it Fonzie decided to get married to a class chick whom he thought was a librarian. In reality, as Richie and Howard discover, she is a stripper. It turns out that she really liked Fonzie but was afraid of losing him if she told him her true profession.

Her fears were justified. The Fonz lives by strict rules, a habit that Henry Winkler is all too aware of. Henry has said that he makes "too many rules for myself."

One of Fonzie's rules was "Never marry a girl who 'does.'" So Fonzie lost the girl, but the audience didn't lose *Happy Days*. All Henry's

The Fonz's second and greatest love, Pinky Tuscedaro!

work and Miller-Marshall's gamble paid off. The live studio audience warmed to The Fonz, and the home audience took to him like honey to a grapefruit. *Happy Days* was a reborn hit!

CULMINATION

In some places the moves that gave *Happy Days* its second lease on life would have caused bitterness and hurt. But the big difference on this set was an entire group who cared. Jerry Paris, their head honcho, used the reorganization to strengthen and develop the characters.

Miller and Marshall made sure that, even though Fonzie was now the center of attention, not one other actor suffered neglect or inconsideration. Now almost anybody can perceive a refreshing change in the show. The episodes are happier, more joyous, and about winning, not losing. And they are overwhelmingly successful. You can tune in now and feel like a part of what is going on without the worry of seeing a downbeat or depressing comedy.

The Fonz signifies strength, success, and, most important, cool. But not a cruel cool. A cool that says it's okay to be different, it's okay to do what's right, not just what's fashionable. It's cool *to be yourself.*

As Jerry Paris puts it in explaining what makes The Fonz tick: "[It's] due to his strong code of ethics based on nonviolence and the Golden Rule."

The rest of the cast echoes like sentiments about the show and their costar, Henry Winkler. Ron Howard was pleased when Henry was given second billing and caught on. Tom Bosley feels good about sharing the show.

Marion Ross knew that Henry was developing with his role and could appreciate his growing pains. She had had a long and rocky career on stage and screen herself, including work on *Blueprint For Robbery* and *Colossus: The Forbin Project*, so she was happy that the changes gave the show a family feel.

Anson Williams was in no position to complain. He was too happy. His underdog characterization was handled with consideration and gentle understanding. The jokes at Potsie's expense were never cruel, and the script occasionally acknowledged the unfairness of his position. The audience roots for Potsie, and the evidence

is obvious in the rest of Anson's professional life. His personal appearances are at a premium and are usually well received. His singing career is developing, and he is in constant demand for game shows and talk shows. Right now Anson is sitting pretty.

Donny Most, by his own admission; " . . . still can't believe all this is happening."

All this is his notoriety, his fan mail, his new album, and his success. He had only been in L.A. a little while before he got roles on *Room 222* and *Emergency*. Then he was suddenly auditioning for the pivotal role of Ralph Malph.

"I auditioned about three times," he said. "A few days later I found out that they wanted me."

Donny is in a good position, since he is now a "name" but at the same time does not portray a role that he's likely to get locked into. He can spread out with little fear of typecasting.

"I feel secure right now . . . but it can fall right out of the sky," he says. But he can still admit that he was "thrilled, surprised, shocked, happy and . . . still excited about everything that's been happening."

The public reaction to the show and to The Fonz soon became massive. Letters poured into the studio for the whole group but mostly for The Fonz. As a matter of fact, it was reported that ninety percent of *all* Paramount's fan mail was for The Fonz.

The studio knew a good thing when it had it and offered to do a spinoff on Fonz. Movie producers wanted to do a film Fonz. Women began writing, begging The Fonz to love them. Soon The Fonz was everywhere. On T-shirts, on blankets, on book covers, on coffee mugs, on notebooks, on buttons, on posters, on board games, and on records. A plastic model was introduced. A movable doll was manufactured, complete with fake leather jacket and a rod that you can push down to make the doll's hands do the thumbs-up sign.

The magazines picked up on The Fonz. Titles soon screamed from the racks: "The Fonz! Why His Sex Techniques Drive Women Crazy!"; "Revealed! How Fonzie Uses Magic Powers to Make Girls Love Him!"; "Fonzie Reveals His True Loves!"

Everything seemed to be Fonz, Fonz, Fonz. And nothing seemed to be Henry Winkler. And,

Off stage, the guy's are great pals. Here they show a little T-shirt flash.

The Cunninghams as they appeared first season, including the rarely seen second brother, Chuck (Randolph Roberts, second from right).

to the inner-directed, confirmed actor, the kind of mindless adulation that his *character* was getting seemed dangerous.

He wasn't The Fonz. The strength and cool that millions were seeing in The Fonz were not in him. But the masses expected and seemed determined to get it from him. He, who had as much in common with The Fonz as football has with ballet. Fear had reentered Henry's life from another direction.

"The spotlight does more than make it bright around you," he explains. "It makes you a target."

The Fonz, to Henry, soon became an almost alien presence. A parasite existing in his body, controlling his actions, but not really him. As a matter of fact, Henry has said: "If I had met The Fonz then [when he was younger], I would have pretended I was blind so he would leave me alone."

Elsewhere he admits to enjoying his success, but at the same time he is worried. He is worried that the huge response to The Fonz will type him and kill his acting career.

"The adulation . . . can turn your head . . . or the fear . . . hits you and tells you that soon it will all be over and you'll be worse off than before you were discovered. That you are, forever, forgotten."

So almost immediately Henry began to create more rules for himself. He took advantage of his fame but in honest Winkler fashion. He spent most of his free time as a public servant. He appeared for charities; he made public-service TV announcements and strove to show his fans, en masse and quickly, that he would rather be loved as Henry Winkler than as The Fonz.

But Henry's most pressing danger is not to be typed as The Fonz. It is himself. While others of his stature and situation take immediate constructive steps to prove their worth and versatility (as John Travolta in *Welcome Back, Kotter*),

Henry thinks, questions, and ponders. Instead of using The Fonz to achieve his goals Henry seems to be trying to soft-pedal himself and wait until reaction dies down before making his move.

His coactors on *Happy Days* have already branched out extensively. Both Anson Williams and Donny Most have put out record albums. Tom Bosley became the host of *Radio Adventure Theater*. Ron Howard not only costarred with John Wayne in *The Shootist*, which reestablished his talent, but also made a deal with the aforementioned Roger Corman. That resulted not only in a starring role in the money-making *Eat My Dust* but also in directing and starring assignments in his father's script, *Grand Theft Auto*.

CONCLUSION

As of this writing Henry has signed to do the motion picture *Heroes*, reportedly a comedy drama about G.I.s returning from Vietnam.

If his role is good enough and if the film is well made, it might do the trick for Henry. But if it doesn't, what then? He has acknowledged the fact that he intends to leave *Happy Days* when his contract runs out two years from now, but instead of riding the wave of his popularity Henry seems to be waiting for the crest to pass by so he can paddle ashore. Whether or not it's a commendable or a wise decision only time will tell.

But once in an interview Henry was asked for some parting advice. He said: "Don't do any bad deeds because you're paid back for all bad karma. Decide what your most important goals are and work hard to achieve them . . . Don't get down on yourself because self-respect is the cornerstone of joy."

Henry Winkler is staying honest with himself, and I don't know about anybody else, but I'm with you, Henry.

The gathered sweathogs learn Kotter's first rule of teaching;
"speak softly and carry a big 'schtick'."

WELCOME BACK, KOTTER

or Four on a Match

Gabe Kaplan as Kotter
Robert Hegyes as Epstein
Lawrence-Hilton Jacobs as Boom-Boom Washington
Ron Palillo as Horshack
John Travolta as Barbarino

James Komack is an interesting man. He seemed to appear almost out of nowhere as coproducer and actor on *The Courtship of Eddie's Father*, the show that was responsible for turning Bill Bixby's career around. Shortly after he blasted into prime time, producing two huge successes.

One was a Norman Lear-lookalike situation comedy. Norman Lear had broken through some of television's restrictive codes with a show called *All in the Family*. Lear followed that up with various relevant comedies about minority groups that were spun off from his previous shows, such as *The Jeffersons* and *Good Times*. His other major success was created in the same way as *Family*, by Americanizing an English BBC-TV show. Lear switched the cockney of *Steptoe and Son* to Afro-American and came up with *Sanford and Son*, starring Redd Foxx.

Komack "borrowed" the concept of a cranky old man and his young coworker from Sanford-Steptoe and introduced Puerto Rican influences instead of Black to create *Chico and the Man*.

The show was to end in tragedy a few years after its creation (more on that later), but Komack's companion program, cut from a more original mold, is still going strong. As a matter of fact, at this writing it is about to give birth to a spanking new baby-boy spinoff.

In 1974 producer Alan Sacks brought a concept and a young comedian to meet Komack. The comedian was a painfully shy, introverted, inarticulate man with the unlikely name of Gabriel Kaplan. The concept concerned a young teacher who manages to get a job teaching problem students at the same school at which he had been a problem student ten years before.

Komack didn't like the comedian and hated the concept. "I thought it was the worst idea I had ever heard," said Komack in an article, "a combination of Mr. Chips and *The Blackboard Jungle*."

But after awhile the possibilities of the series became apparent. A.B.C. was slowly working its way to the top of the network heap, chiefly on the strength of its youthful audience. A.B.C. had a near-monopoly of teenage idols, who controlled the airways, the magazine racks, and almost this entire book. A.B.C. had spots available on their schedule, and they wanted shows that would be meaningful to their audience. And what could be more meaningful to kids in school than kids in school?

Komack also began to see what Kaplan and Sacks had known all along. The series' premise had an inherent ability to say something meaningful to its audience. To deliver a message to young people via young people. And one thing Komack was a caring producer. One has only to watch *Eddie's Father* or *Chico* to see his consideration for the characters and the audience. So he went ahead and became the executive producer of a show called *Welcome Back, Kotter*.

The show premiered in 1975 but didn't take off immediately. It was doing well but was up against *The Waltons*, which was hearty family viewing. *Kotter* was followed by *Barney Miller*, which the network brass considered a very "ungrabbing" show. A.B.C.s Thursday family-hour lineup was in jeopardy.

But *The Waltons* had already been on for a few seasons. It seemed that its wholesome happiness was beginning to wear thin on its viewers. Add to that the fact that *Barney Miller* had some pretty strong defenders both at home and at the network. So they were given time to rework their production into a better show. And, finally, add to all the preceding the fact that A.B.C. had not really given the discerning young viewer an alternative to *The Waltons*, and you've got the makings of a major media upset.

Audiences began to discover *Welcome Back, Kotter* and *Barney Miller*. They soon fled Walton's Mountain in droves to settle into a rundown high school in Brooklyn, New York, with its tempting attractions.

Those tempting attractions went by the names of Gabe Kaplan and, in alphabetical order, Robert Hegyes, Lawrence Hilton Jacobs, Ron Palillo, and John Travolta (please, no screaming).

Rarely does a show come along that smacks so much of a team effort. As soon as you decide one week that Gabe Kaplan is the star of the show, next week along comes Ron Palillo. Then the week after that John Travolta. Then the week after—well, you get the picture.

These four gentlemen happily share the spotlight. Gabe Kaplan has even admitted publicly that he owes all his success to the kids on the show. But at the same time they owe all their success to Gabe for creating their characters and seeing the show through. Who is this quadrangle of talent plus one? What makes their ensemble work so well that they can shine individually? A look into each of their careers may provide a clue.

GABE KAPLAN

I've already asked a couple of questions about the *Kotter* crew, so I might as well ask one more. What drives a man so much that he is willing to give up his love life, any thought of another career, and his own health to pursue the life of a comedian? Answer: don't ask me; ask Gabe Kaplan. He's the one who is doing just that. He's the one who is risking life and limb, not so much for the money but for the recognition, for the fame. Because that's a comedian's goal. To make as many people as possible laugh. And to get paid for it.

A fascinating possibility is evident when one surveys Gabe's life. The key to his obsession might be found in the very place that he has made famous every week on television. A Brooklyn high school.

Because Gabe Kaplan grew up in Brooklyn and went to Erasmus High School for an education. Not his education, *an* education. An education in characters and types. Gabe learned more about people and about how to stay alive than he did about reading, writing, and arithmetic.

Many educators still feel that the person who you are to become is greatly molded during the high-school years. The key to the intense "workaholic" (as he calls himself) might just be found there.

Gabe was born on March 31 in the Crown Heights section of Brooklyn, the son of a real-estate salesman and a beautician. As he grew up in his tough environment and before the natural puberty development could take place (aided by peers and parents), Gabe retreated into the shell of fantasy.

He would go to comedies in the movie theaters. The classics: Laurel and Hardy, Charlie Chaplin, and Buster Keaton, as well as the more recent hits of Abbott and Costello, the Marx Brothers, and Jerry Lewis.

He would watch TV. Sid Caesar on *Your Show of Shows*. Ernie Kovacs and his magnificent sight gags. Milton Berle and the "anything goes" style of comedy. Steve Allen and the whole wacky crew of Don Knotts, Bill Dana, Tom Poston, Gabe Dell, Louie Nye, and Martha Raye on the original *Tonight Show*. Red Skelton and Phil Silvers as Sgt. Bilko.

The big three: Robert Hegyes as Epstein, Lawrence Hilton Jacobs as Washington, and John Travolta as Barbarino.

All were there, cascading across his mind. His parents knew from his I.Q. tests that he was very intelligent, but the energy that he should have been allotting for his schoolwork he was spending on studying the master comedians.

His interest in humor grew and grew until he was not content to sit in his living room or in the theaters, so he started seeking out little hole-in-the-wall nightclubs, large expensive resorts, coffee houses, anywhere that he could find a live comedian.

Meanwhile, Gabe's self-consumption was turning off his fellow students. His inability to relate to their world of broads, fun, sports, and booze made high school a trial for him. Like the character of Horshack that he was later to create, Gabe pulled back his natural intelligence but felt too inhibited to be a class clown. Soon he had had enough.

Even though he had harbored thoughts of becoming a teacher, he dropped out of school in his senior year when the opportunity of becoming a minor-league baseball player beckoned.

A minor league baseball player? Gabe Kaplan? Well, yes and no. After awhile the management of the team found out what Gabe already knew. That he was not cut out for the life of a ballplayer. Even though he was placed, aptly enough, way out in left field, Gabe was soon cut from the squad.

Uncomfortable with the thought of returning to school, Gabe drifted from job to job, all the while feeding his passion for humor and comedians. Finally, he found a position that would give him bread-and-butter money while still allowing him the opportunity to hone his comedy craft. Gabe went to work as a bellboy in a New Jersey hotel.

Night after night he watched the comedians whom the hotel brought in to entertain the guests. Time after time he studied their timing, their material, their moves. Finally, he decided to try to make his way on his own as a comedian.

His parents and what friends he had knew Gabe to be an honest and decent fellow. They just couldn't understand what was driving him to enter the seamy substrata of nightclub comedians.

"You're throwing your life away," he was told, "You're beating your brains out for nothing."

SWEATHOGS

John Travolta

Born: February 18, 1954

Place of Birth: Englewood, New Jersey

Parents: Salvatore and Helen Burke Travolta

Nationality: Italian

Educated: Dwight Morrow High School

Films: *The Devil's Rain* (with William Shatner)
Carrie (with Sissy Spacek)
The Boy in the Plastic Bubble (with Glynnis O'Connor)

Plays: *Grease*
Over Here

Height: 6' 0"

Weight: 170 pounds

Eyes: Blue

Hair: Brown

Hobbies: Flying, cars

Address: c/o *Welcome Back, Kotter*
Prospect at Talmadge
Hollywood, Cal. 90027
or
Sweathogs
ABC-TV
4151 Prospect Ave.
Los Angeles, Cal. 90027

Lawrence-Hilton Jacobs

Born: September 4,

Place of Birth: New York City

Parents: Hilton and Clothilda Jacobs

Nationality: Afro-American

Educated: Manhattan High School of Art
and Design
Al Fann Theatrical Ensemble
New York Negro Ensemble

Films: *Death Wish* (with Charles Bronson)
Serpico (with Al Pacino)
The Gambler (with James Caan)
Claudine (with James Earl Jones)
Cooley High
Sojourner

Height: 6' 2½"   Weight: 163 pounds

Eyes: Brown   Hair: Brown

Hobbies: Art, music

Robert Hegyes

Born: May 7,

Place of Birth: Perth Amboy, New Jersey

Parents: Steven and Marie Hegyes

Nationality: Italian Hungarian

Educated: Metuchen High School
Wilkes College
Glassboro State College

Plays: *Naomi Court*
Don't Look Back

Film: *Dog Day Afternoon* (with Al Pacino)

Height: 5' 7½"   Weight: 160 pounds

Eyes: Brown   Hair: Black

Hobbies: Golf, baseball

Ron Pallilo

Born: April 2,

Place of Birth: New Haven, Connecticut

Parents: Gabriel and Carmel Pallilo

Nationality: Italian

Educated: University of Connecticut

Plays: *A Midsummer Night's Dream*
Summer Brave
Hot L Baltimore
The Last Sweet Days Of Isaac

Height: 5' 7"   Weight: 120 pounds

Eyes: Hazel   Hair: Brown

Hobbies: Running, swimming, reading, art

Gabe was too insecure even to try to be accepted into the struggling comedian community. While people such as Robert Klein, Albert Brooks, and David Brenner were getting jobs and rising in the business, club owners didn't know Gabe from Adam.

Even while this heartbreaking existence was going on, Gabe was sharpening his act and timing. Even while he worked as an M.C. at strip joints, he was working to improve himself artistically. Finally, his routine was so shiny that it sparkled in sunlight. He practically dripped wit. He was ready. Gabe managed to show his stuff at the Comedy Workshop in New York.

The word got around. The guy is good. Soon Gabe was getting work at the better nightclubs. Then Johnny Carson extended an invitation to *The Tonight Show*, a spot that has made or broken many a newcoming comedian. Thankfully, Gabe was still good, and his initial TV appearance led to spots on other talk and variety shows.

Finally, he was signed to do warmup spots at Las Vegas hotels and to a record contract. Gabe made an album of his routines called *Holes and Mellow Rolls*. The cover was of a couple of missile-shaped melting ice-cream bars rocketing across a colorful background.

Gabe had finally started on the road to success, with routines on Ed Sullivan's guest list, satires of TV shows such as *Kung Fu*, the "nervous pleasures of pubescent sex," and, most important, tales of his teachers and fellow students in Brooklyn.

But even though he seemed to be doing well, his slowly rising career stalled. His record album wasn't successful, and he wasn't getting the recognition that a comedian with his credits deserved.

Perhaps the new young audiences wanted more fast-talking stream-of-consciousness comedians such as Richard Pryor or George Carlin. Whatever the reasons, Gabe Kaplan's clipped, laid-back delivery and mannered material wasn't catching on.

Suddenly a not-so-natural extension of his craft opened up to him. An A.B.C. producer suggested that he develop his routines about Brooklyn into a TV-series conception. So Gabe got together with Alan Sacks, also a graduate of Erasmus High, and started to piece together his memories.

Horshack, Epstein, Barbarino, and Washington were created as representative types, patterned after real people whom Gabe used to know. The Kotter character himself was based on a female teacher whom he remembered. She "cared and had ways to reach students," Gabe has said about her. Then he married his Kotter character to give him "stability and morality," as Kaplan puts it, and introduced a basic conflict of "old-style" vs. "new-style" teaching through a sourpuss vice principal named Mr. Woodman.

The finished package was then delivered to James Komack and—well, you already know that story. Success! The key to all Gabe's dreams was realized. Fame, club offers, dates came flooding toward him. After years of hard work Gabe finally had the opportunity to sit back, relax, and savor the fruits of his labor.

Gabe Kaplan? Sit back and relax? No way! That's like The Fonz showing up for a date in a three-piece pinstripe suit! Gabe's way of savoring his success was to take advantage of every opportunity that he possibly could. For the first time in his life he had the opportunity to communicate his favorite way, nonstop.

"My image is to be a funny, together, outgoing person," he said in an article. "But I'm not like that. I'm inhibited and shy. I'm only me when I'm performing."

And even though he loves people, especially kids, he says in another article: "I have less time for romance now than I did when I was on the road." And in still another: "I don't have time to make friends or meet people or do anything."

But Gabe seems to like it that way. He seems to be doing what he likes best. Working. Working maniacally. His present schedule sees him working from 10:00 A.M. to 5:00 P.M. at the A.B.C. studios, jetting to Las Vegas for two club gigs at 8:00 P.M. and midnight, then flying back to L.A. for the next day's *Kotter* work. And this is in addition to his guest commitments and recording his next album!

Now what about the gang that Gabe feels is responsible for making his sitcom the hit that it is? Here, in alphabetical order, come the sweathogs!

Gabe Kaplan as Kotter looks like he's auditioning for martyrdom when dealing with Epstein.

ROBERT HEGYES

Juan Luis Pedro Phillippo de Huevos Epstein. Say that five times fast. Robert Hegyes can. Because he is Juan Luis Pedro Phillippo de Huevos Epstein. At least to millions of fans every Thursday night.

Everybody who watches knows what Epstein is like. The eternal huckster, he's the guy who could buy four hubcaps from you in the morning and sell them back to you at a twenty-dollar profit in the afternoon. He's a guy who could get out of a test with a forged note one day and sell you the answers to that same test the next.

But how about Robert Hegyes? Could it be that he was like the character that he portrays in high school? You bet your microscopic crib sheet he was! The only difference seemed to be that Bob went to high school in Perth Amboy, New Jersey instead of Brooklyn and that he's actually Italian Hungarian instead of Puerto Rican.

The similarities were intense and numerous. "I had the potential to be a really good student," Robert says, "but the motivation wasn't there."

It seems that an "unfortunate conflict" with an elementary grade-school teacher left him with a sour taste in his mouth about organized education. So, even while he developed as an individual, he had little but disdain for school. Robert seemed to subscribe to the Mark Twain quotation, "I never let my schooling get in the way of my education."

"I wasn't lazy," says Robert. "I just had it in my head that I had better things to do."

His education alienation continued through high school, where he would indulge in such sundry dealings as finding someone in the class before his to get the upcoming answers, getting his guidance counselor to schedule his classes so that he had no math or science, and going to summer school to pass present math tests.

In between his intrigues Robert continued to broaden his creative horizons. Besides developing his acting skills he joined the high-school band as a drummer.

So Robert was having fun, honing his skills, and looking forward to a life of "either a very well-disciplined academician . . . or an itinerant . . . hobo."

But when he began his first year of college, all his preconceptions were given a good shaking up.

"I really paid the price," he admits.

At Wilkes College in Wilkes-Barre, Pennsylvania, a small university where a not-so-good student can continue a quality education, Robert flunked biology and suffered through a year of not knowing the subjects or how to properly prepare for them.

"I really had to learn how to study all over again," he said. But it wasn't all depression and fear of flunking. Robert also met a young blonde girl named Mary Eileen Kunes. They fell in love and were married in September 1973. By that time Robert's natural intelligence and gentle aggressiveness had surfaced, and he went on to graduate from another college with a Bachelor of Arts (B.A.) degree in speech and theater education.

"I started out to be a teacher," says Robert. "But I found the format of high school inflexible. You can't teach acting like you can teach history."

But Robert stuck it out for awhile, doing substitute and student teaching while Mary worked in New York in her chosen field, microbiology. Finally, the urge to act became too much for him. He went directly to New York to pursue a theatrical career—do not pass go, do not collect two hundred dollars. And he didn't either. Collect two hundred dollars, I mean. He managed to get work but sometimes for nothing and sometimes for as little as twenty dollars a show.

But Mary was still working, so the Hegyes at least had financial security. "There is constant rejection when you go . . . to find work as an actor," Robert explained. "As determined as I thought I was, it was Mary who kept lifting me up . . . and sending me . . . out the door the next day."

Robert made his mark off-Broadway, as a dangerous young hood in *Naomi Court*. On Broadway Robert made his mark as a dangerous young hood in *Don't Call Back*, a short-lived thriller with Arlene Francis. In the movies Robert worked as an extra in *Dog Day Afternoon* with Al Pacino, John Cazale, and Charles Durning. So all that he had left to do in order to experience all the acting media was to appear on television. And, of course, he accomplished that in a rather spectacular fashion.

Kotter and Epstein exaggerate their concern over an emotional Barbarino.

Mary and Robert talked over his decision to move out to California after they were informed that Robert was one of four out of five hundred auditionees chosen to play a sweathog on *Welcome Back, Kotter*. They both agreed that it was an opportunity not to be ignored. Even if the show flopped, it would be a good credit on his resume and a great experience. So Mary happily left her secure job at the New York laboratory; they packed their cat, Selma-Kato, and their dog, Reefer; and headed west in the Hegyes van.

Now we all know what happened, don't we? The show and the stars were a hit, steadily climbing the Nielsen charts until they reached the top ten. But the fast fame and money has not unduly affected Robert Hegyes. The supposed glamor of Hollywood didn't dazzle him: he seemed to take it right in stride. He and Mary seem as happy as ever, and no sooner did they get to the West Coast than they set up a home in Burbank and started decorating.

The Hegyes have taken to the rest of the *Kotter* crew like family; Robert is universally considered the most level-headed of them all, and Mary has become a best friend to all the sweathogs.

"And besides everything else," Ron Palillo was reported to have said, "she's a good cook. When we get an invite for dinner, you can bet we're not late!"

Robert sums up his ability to accustom himself to almost anything in this way: "People might talk about the dues I've paid to get where I am . . . [but] the fact of the matter is I could have never done it without Mary. She's the one who deserves the credit . . . and if my career ever begins to interfere with our marriage, I'll chuck the career just that fast. That's where my . . . priority is. Not on any soundstage."

That's what it's all about, Robert. That's the only reason there is.

LAWRENCE HILTON JACOBS

It all looks so easy from where we, the audience, sit. One day a new show premieres; we either like it or we don't; we watch it grow from week to week; and then, all of a sudden, we begin to either love or envy the people on screen.

"Look at that girl in the back row. She gets to sit behind Barbarino!" "Wouldn't it be great if I could do that?" "The lucky stiff. He gets to have fun and gets lots of money, too. Week after week."

Is it that easy? Does someone just wander into a hit show? Well, maybe one incredibly lucky person out of five million but not on the *Kotter* set. Everyone there has paid his dues and is dedicated to the craft of acting.

Especially Lawrence Hilton Jacobs. The mystery man. The man who plays the lanky, easygoing future basketball star, Boom-Boom Washington. Who is Larry Jacobs? Beyond that question, who is Boom-Boom Washington? Of the whole *Kotter* crowd he seems to be the most nebulous, the least drawn out. We know that he's tall, Black, good-looking, smart, and a premier sweathog, but, beyond his sotto-voce "Hi, there," we don't know where he comes from, who his parents are, or what his life is like.

Well, you won't find all the above true about Lawrence Hilton Jacobs. At least not in my book. Larry Jacobs was the fifth of nine children sired by Hilton and Clothilda Jacobs in the Big Apple, New York City. And from the very beginning his parents' love and guidance helped him to discover himself as a person.

"They always taught us to work for what we wanted," Jacobs said. "To pay our bills and do everything in our power to keep the family together."

With that important lesson in mind, what made the young man suddenly see an acting career as his lifelong goal?

"I was attracted to acting. I don't know," he said, "maybe it was a TV show. Or a live show or whatever. All I know is that from my earliest memories I thought of nothing but going into this work."

Other sources bear out this dream of Larry's. In interviews and articles Larry almost always answers the question in the same way: "I've always wanted to be an actor."

But that's not to say that he didn't have any other interests as a young man. No good actor can afford to shut out the rest of the world. Two major influences on him were art and music. Art became so interesting to him that he spent many of his teen years at the Manhattan High School of Art and Design, learning fine and applied art, developing his skills for commercial work.

He used his talents as a draftsman soon after,

Hal Linden and Abe Vigoda, of "Barney Miller," on the right.
Along with the sweathogs, they have "locked up"
ABC's Thursday night line-up.

as he began to move into the theatrical world. A young actor must eat, so Larry worked with a fashion designer and a package designer and a freelance artist, not to mention various other sundry occupations, to keep the bread coming in.

The money he made, he reports, went for acting lessons. "When you want something bad enough, you really go all out," he's said.

Larry's other creative interest was music. He took a great love of the keyboards and applied it, learning to play the piano by ear and composing his own works. When asked what he wanted to be if not an actor, Larry answered, "A composer." Reportedly, he still wants to score the music for major motion pictures someday.

So the young Lawrence Hilton Jacobs occupied a stream of positions as he chased his elusive goal of making a living in the theater. Messenger, stockroom man, gas-station attendant, department-store employee, flower-store worker, and the occasional modeling job or commercial.

Finally, on the strength of his acting ability Larry got into the Al Fann Theatrical Ensemble and from there got involved with the famous New York Negro Ensemble Company. He played his roles honestly, charmingly, and strongly.

Soon his merits were recognized outside the theater. He copped small roles in *The Gambler* with James Caan, *Death Wish* with Charles Bronson, and *Serpico* with Al Pacino, all New York-based films, but his real notoriety in the business came with his supporting role as Diahann Carroll's militant son in *Claudine* and with his leading role as a jiving, cocky, future basketball player in *Cooley High* (sounds like a certain sweathog we all know, doesn't it?).

For the most part, in *Claudine* Larry wasn't reviewed as much as acknowledged. His role was forceful, and his work was always mentioned but usually not with his off-screen name included. For instance, one critic said, "Claudine's oldest son is dead set against her marrying the garbage man," while another just blanketed all the supporting roles by saying, "The rest of the film is, like, meticulously casted." Then the critic goes on to give away the rest of the plot.

But *Cooley High* was another story. Released into theaters in the summer of 1975 as an "answer" to *American Graffiti, Time Magazine* said that it had "all the grace of an army training film . . . [but it] . . . does have [an] energetic performance by Lawrence Hilton Jacobs."

Newsweek was a little less restrained. "Script is clumsily plotted . . . plays for cheap laughs . . . but Lawrence Hilton Jacobs [is] wonderful."

In the film Larry played Cochise, a basketball star who is hoping for an athletic scholarship to get out of the ghetto. He achieves it only to be beaten almost to death by a gang of toughs because of a misunderstanding.

After his success in that film Larry went to the West Coast to visit for three days. He stayed for ten. Because at that time A.B.C. was auditioning for a new show that they had tentatively entitled *Kotter.* Larry read and then went back to New York. But once he arrived, he was called back to California to film the pilot of *Welcome Back, Kotter.*

"I still can't believe how it all happened," says Jacobs.

But Larry wasn't always that happy. At first he worried about what effect Boom-Boom Washington would have on his life. Could a television role following some moderate movie success burn out his career? Larry is a serious actor, not just a joe out for a good time, so this was a serious consideration. But when he looked around at the talented actors who could star on TV and in films, actors such as James Earl Jones (a costar in *Claudine*), Bill Cosby (*Uptown Saturday Night*), Ben Vereen(*Funny Lady*), and Lou Gossett (*The Deep*), he realized that Boom-Boom could only do to him what he let it.

"See, man," he explained, "we're all insecure, every actor is, and, when that insecurity has success mounted on top of it, it can boggle your mind."

But now Lawrence Hilton Jacobs is in Hollywood and in a hit and he loves it. Not only does *Kotter* open up another world of opportunity for him to spread out and to try other things as well as effectively using his art and musical talents, but he also has time for other favorite pastimes. Such as sports. And reading, an enthusiasm that he shares with the entire *Kotter* cast. Larry, like the other dedicated actors on *Kotter,* maintains the honest wish to become a better actor and person.

"The acting business is hard, and it takes a great deal of mental work."

"And I think anyone who says success hasn't changed them isn't being truthful. It does change you, and usually you're not even aware of it."

Larry's trying to stay aware of it and making sure that any change is for the better.

RON PALILLO

There are four sweathogs. But if you played a game of "one of these things is not like the others" with them, there would be only three. It's obvious when you look at all four that one is totally different from the others. One isn't quite handsome. One isn't quite tall. One isn't quite independent. One is, in temperament and style, really quite weird.

His name is Arnold Horshack. Ar-nold Horshack. Even the name doesn't sound together. And, because of Horshack's difference, he and the young man who plays him stand out.

Arnold is more intelligent but weaker than the other three, and in a tough Brooklyn high school brains and a quarter won't even get you a ride on the subway anymore. So Arnold, short, sweet, nasal-toned Arnold, choked down his intelligence and put his wit in overdrive. Through his bouncy ability to be an underdog with style Horshack was accepted as a sweathog, with all the prestige and protection that accompanied such a position.

The character of Horshack is brassy, kinky, and mannered. He has adopted several methods of communication that have become his trademarks. These are, of course, his hacking, whinnying laugh and the "ooh, ooh, ooh," that orchestrates any hand raising. It is the talents of the Connecticut-born and -bred Ron Palillo that keep Horshack from crossing the line of character into caricature. He comes pretty darn close sometimes, but he never quite crosses it.

Ron was born in New Haven, Connecticut, the home of Yale, where Henry Winkler went to school. Ron was one of three boys and one girl born to Gabriel and Carmel Palillo, an Italian family living in the town of Cheshire. Mr. Palillo was a postmaster, and the missus was a furrier as well as a part-time waitress.

Their town, like other Connecticut towns such as Woodbridge, Bethany, and Orange, was small, rustic, leafy, and comfortable. Many historic old homes lined the curving country roads in these towns, and the usually mild weather created an idyllic setting for the dreamer that Ron Palillo was to become.

While his older brothers and sister continued their educations in preparation for careers in teaching, medicine, and science, Ron fantasized about a life in acting. He got the bug from his parents, both of whom had a great love of the theater and reportedly would bring the little Ron to as many stage productions as they could.

When he was nine, Mr. Palillo died, making life very difficult for the whole family. Everyone worked to keep going, including Ron. But what could a small boy who dreamed of acting do? Why, start a theater, of course! A theater? When he was not even old enough to shave? Sure, why not?

"My family always believed," Ron said, "that the best way to make a dream come true is to work for it."

So Ron, hardly into high school, learned more about the theater than most people learn in four years of college. How? Not just by reading but by actually opening his own theater.

"I got to play all the parts that I ever wanted to," Ron reports. "I was the director, the producer, the publicity man . . . You name it, I did it."

The fourteen-year-old Palillo named it The Black Friars Summer Theater, after one of Shakespeare's early English stages, and made it a financial and artistic success. By then he had entered high school and the world of appearances, peers, responsibility, and cliques. Even there his romanticized love of King Arthur, Shakespeare, and the theater held him in good stead. For, like Horshack, Ron wasn't too good-looking and didn't have the hypocrisy to try to fit into a world of jocks and cheerleaders.

"I was four foot eight until I was seventeen," Ron will tell you.

So he went back to the theater and spent most of his days working on and in shows, since his peers and teachers gave him very little motivation to do anything else. College provided some heavy acceleration. Ron applied and was admitted to the University of Connecticut, where he majored in theater. There he met his acting and directing teacher, a man named Mr. Katter (no, there's no spelling mistake; yes, that's his real name).

"He taught me techniques and educated me to be a professional," Ron says. "Mr. Katter also insisted I train in Shakespeare."

It is hard to shake off the funny picture of Ron Palillo doing *Hamlet* with the Arnold Horshack speech and mannerisms, but the fact of the matter is that Ron performed professionally in incredibly difficult productions such as *Shakespeare's Other Side of Love*. Ron toured in this two-person show, performing scenes from *Richard III, The Taming of the Shrew, Macbeth,* and other plays depicting the less famous of the Bard's love scenes. The scenes depicting selfish love, destructive love, jealous love, and mad love. I know a few people who would go into catatonic shock if they saw their beloved Horshack doing that (I, for one, wouldn't mind).

After graduating from UConn, Ron took up residence in Greenwich Village, New York, or the East Village, as he calls it. Greenwich Village is one of the few Bohemian areas left. It is walled in by the human refuse of Avenues A and B on one side and by the middle-class midtown rush of Fourteenth Street on the other. But the East Village itself practically thrives with creativity. Wall to wall it is crawling with artists, musicians, interns, poets, writers, and actors trying to make their way. The dirty streets and the slightly run-down brownstones hum with creativity, frustrated and constructive alike. There Ron Palillo began to make connections and play professional roles.

He did *A Midsummer Night's Dream* with Mickey Rooney. He went on tour with both *Richard III* and William Inge's *Summer Brave*. He did summer stock. He did repertory theater. He appeared in *Twelfth Night, Hello, Dolly,* and *Macbeth,* among others.

And throughout his experiences he managed to hold onto his romanticism and natural effervescence. That certain thing in Ron that makes him give his all, no matter what role he portrays.

Ron was soon chosen to play the lead in *The Last Sweet Days of Isaac* on educational TV, a part that Austin Pendleton created on Broadway. From that job Ron managed to secure a part in the famous Circle in the Square Theater's original production of *The Hot L Baltimore.*

He had been in that for a year when the casting call came for *Kotter.* As Ron tells it: "I thought I was wrong for the part . . . I read the script, and I didn't think it was funny."

But then he decided to read the part with his Brooklynese accent, the one that Horshack is now known for on the show. Ron still professes that he didn't know why he chose to take such a gamble, but it obviously worked. He had Gabe Kaplan and Alan Sacks laughing almost right away. By the end of the audition they knew that they wanted Ron.

The vulnerability, the cuteness, and the uniqueness of Ron's Horshack came through loud and clear to the millions watching *Welcome Back, Kotter.* Girls wanted to mother him, and mothers thanked him for helping their own children adjust to not being able to fit in.

Ron is still a romantic and almost unbearably cute. His happy little cherub smile is in evidence everywhere. His "love me—I'm sincere" expression either makes one faint or drives one crazy. "Adorable" pictures of Ron in big floppy hats or on the phone or holding his furry dogs Arnold and Fred or on a New York rooftop or cuddling a tree adorn all the articles about him.

What makes him perform so much? Why is he so willing to give so much of Horshack all the time?

"I made a vow . . . when I was . . . fourteen . . . that it was always going to be for the audience . . . Everything I do is really for the audience. I would just [like to] . . . thank them and tell them that it's all for them, really."

Well, even the most cynical of us can't argue with that.

JOHN TRAVOLTA

Vinnie Barbarino. Stop screaming, girls. You know Vinnie Barbarino, don't you? I said, stop screaming, girls! Vinnie Barbarino—girls, this is the last time I'm going to warn you. Ahem. Vinnie Barbarino is the supermacho, supercool, tough-talking superjock in *Welcome Back, Kotter* (heck, we're not talking about *The Man from U.N.C.L.E.,* y'know).

And the man who plays him has created a nationwide shakeup worthy of the great San Francisco earthquake. If the big earthquakes get an eight on the Richter scale, John Travolta must be getting at least a twenty-five!

The proud group in the classroom to welcome back Kotter.

But John Travolta isn't Barbarino. He, like all the other fan favorites, is just a good actor playing a role. But a big difference between John and all the others is that he's not emphasizing the difference. He doesn't mind being Vinnie. Vinnie doesn't worry him. While many others worry and ponder the question of typecasting, John just goes about his normal business, thereby eliminating the problem of typecasting better than anyone!

Because John's normal business is creating and taking opportunities that beckon. On the day that he finished his first movie, he read for *Kotter*. Shortly after getting the Barbarino role he signed for *Carrie*. In *Carrie* he plays a tough, macho juvenile delinquent in high school. But you don't hear anybody yelling that he was just doing Barbarino, do you?

One good reason was because he wasn't (doing Barbarino). Another good reason is John Travolta's ambition. It is: "to be the best actor I can be and play in every sort of vehicle . . . as long as I believe in what I'm doing. I know that it can only be of help to me. Never anything else."

All right. We return to the treatise that I've started out with every time so far. What makes this man what he is? Why is this twenty-three-year-old high-school dropout so together?

For the answer come back with me into the far reaches of the fifties, back, back, back—excuse me, I think I'm getting sort of punchy. To the point: John Travolta was born February 18, 1954 in Englewood, New Jersey to Salvatore and Helen Burke Travolta.

Mr. Travolta was a Catholic semipro athlete who now owns a tire shop in Hillsdale. Mrs. Travolta is a retired actress and drama coach (what a coincidence!). John was the last of six children, all of whom are now involved in the creative arts. Ellen, his oldest sister, was born in 1940, followed by Sam, Margaret, Ann, and Joe. Ellen is married and has children, is living in California, and at this writing has just gotten a great new job! More about that later. Sam and Joe live in New Jersey and are working on a musical act. Margaret is a Chicago actress, and Ann a New York one. The whole family was and is affected by their parents' goodness and talent.

"They gave us confidence," said John in an article. "We were the best . . . this energy came out of us as creative talent."

And it didn't take long, either. By the time that John got into elementary school, he was joining his mom at rehearsals that she was involved in as an actress, director, or coach.

"As a kid," John remembered, "I'd mimic the actors in all the musical comedies on Broadway."

In such a creative environment John graduated from copying to original performing almost before he knew it. He joined his mother in the play *Who Will Save the Plowboy* at the age of twelve. By the time he was fifteen, he had been happily crammed full of drama, movement, and voice lessons. He was so professional that he was steadily getting stock work and was picked up by an agent when he was sixteen. The "it only happens to other guys" happened to him almost implausibly easily.

Meanwhile, though, another side of John's life was slowly deteriorating. Even though he was ready and eager to work in supermarkets and furniture stores to support himself in his quest for an acting career, one thing was holding him back. School.

High school, to be exact. All the homework, all the classwork, all the subjects not only seemed nonconstructive to the talented Travolta but *anti*constructive. They were weighing him down.

"My friends . . . thought I was a bit off because I was interested in the theater," John explained in an article. "How could I share my kind of experience? I'd have such pain, I'd be crying."

So, weighing what he felt and what he needed against what society seemed to call for, John made a decision.

"I felt that if I were going to make my career in acting . . . the best preparation I could have . . . would be . . . lots of personal on-the-job experience."

Knowing, however, how important an education was, even to an acting career, John came up with an intelligent alternative to quitting school completely.

"I would make a bargain with my parents that if I didn't succeed in my career in a year's time, I'd go back to school."

His parents, seeing the wiseness of such a move and realizing how much John wanted and needed it, gave their consent. So John Travolta

John Travolta as he appeared in the award winning horror movie, "Carrie."

was out of school and on his own with a lot of pressures but also a lot of determination. And his agent served him well. John moved rapidly from summer stock to over thirty TV commercials. From there he got a couple of parts in off-Broadway shows.

Even with all the hustle and bright lights John wisely concentrated on improving himself. He read books, magazines, newspapers; he went to theatrical lectures; he kept his eyes and ears open. He started taking dancing lessons and was even known to wander the streets, studying different types of people in order to remember their actions and reactions.

Soon he drifted out to L.A., where he made the extra-guest-star rounds on shows such as *Emergency* and *Owen Marshall*. He also managed to get a role in the satanic horror film *The Devil's Rain* with Ernest Borgnine and William Shatner of *Star Trek* fame (more about that later). On the final day of filming, as I said, he got the word to read for *Kotter*.

So it seemed that John had it made. He was on a TV show and had proven to everyone that he was a success. So now he could just slum it, right? Well, if you read the Gabe Kaplan section, you'd know that that was a trick question. No, sir. John had the background and the theatrical knowledge to know that a television show wasn't an end in itself.

The show would be cancelled someday, and, even if it wasn't for decades, John the actor didn't want to be Barbarino all his life. So what did he do? Did he deny the Barbarino character? Did he refuse to answer if people called him Vinnie on the street? Did he pull his hair in anguish whenever a girl swooned over his character?

No. He kept working. He chose two movies, one for TV, one destined for theaters, that he liked and did them. He decided that his voice was good enough and, on the strength of his network fame, signed a recording contract and made an album. His hunches paid off.

Carrie was released to a flood of genre interest and then a wave of shocked controversy. Brian DePalma's (*Obsession, Phantom of the Paradise, Sisters*) filmed version of Stephen King's (*Salem's Lot, The Shining*) black fairy tale about a girl who could move things with her mind was a hit! And it couldn't have been better, because a majority of the people who went to see

it didn't see it for John Travolta. They saw it because it was a good movie.

Then *The Boy in the Plastic Bubble,* an A.B.C. television movie, was aired to a large Nielsen rating. John's performance as a young man doomed to spend his life inside a sterile environment because he was born without natural immunities was excellent. And people saw it. They may have tuned in for Barbarino, but they saw John Travolta.

His album came out. Even though he admits that he was performing at "one-quarter of my ability," the record sold well, and two singles from it, *Let Her In* and *Whenever I'm Away From You,* even better.

Finally in late 1976 the word was in. Vinnie Barbarino had surpassed The Fonz in popular acclaim. John's fan mail topped the ten-thousand-a-week mark, and his fans' reaction was collectively humongous. Salvatore Travolta noticed that hunks of the house began to disappear. Phone calls from all over the country at all times of the day and night began to assail the Travolta household. John was mobbed wherever he went. One story goes that the last time he went to a club, women began pawing him and pinching his derrière.

"I felt like a piece of meat!" John said afterwards.

But at the same time he now realizes that it's all part of the job. "I love acting and I do appreciate my fans," he says. "I guess it's the price you have to pay."

John is paying very little and practically painlessly.

ALL TOGETHER NOW

Welcome Back, Kotter. Due to the strength of a variety of individuals it hit the big time, and, with continued wise decisions, it should stay there. Because it has a style, an ability to take five people's strong talents and make an entertaining whole.

Kaplan, Hegyes, Jacobs, Palillo, Travolta, even Marcia Strassman and John Sylvester White have more than just their characterizations to offer. Each has other talents as an individual to explore.

Gabe has wit and an almost desperate need to entertain. Even though he began as what James

John Travolta alone: On your marks, get set, swoon.

Komack calls "the most impossible, confused, uneducated actor I had ever seen," Gabe worked practically twenty-four hours a day developing his ability and getting to know everything he could about the art of television until he made Kotter a strong character on the screen.

Robert Hegyes, with the face of, well, the face of a satanic angel, moves with consummate charm in his role as Epstein.

Lawrence Hilton Jacobs has his dramatic, athletic, artistic, and musical talents to fall back on and could switch directions at any moment.

Ron Palillo, on the basis of public reaction to Horshack, has been given his own spinoff show, *Horshack,* with John Travolta's sister Ellen as Mrs. Horshack, Arnold's mother.

And John Travolta himself, devilish worker and multitalented star, has signed a million-dollar contract for three major motion pictures with the Robert Stigwood organization. The first will be called *Saturday Night* and is about the swinging singles' bar scene; it will be followed by the movie version of *Grease.*

And the show. Through it Kaplan and the crew were able to get across to the people who needed it most important lessons about being a teenager today. Different episodes dealt with work-study, misleading guidance counselors, scholarships, substitute teachers, and even faked pregnancy. But all seemed to have a basic theme in mind. That you've got to be willing to be yourself and to share with other people. That you've got to respect the other guy as a person. And that you've got to be willing to learn. Because that's the only way you'll grow.

On opposite page:
On the left, Marcia Strassman as Julie Kotter and,
on the right, John Sylvester White as Mr. Woodman.

Knock, knock.
Who's there?
STARSKY AND HUTCH.

Starsky and Hutch who? Don't play games. Open up. It's the police!

David Soul as Hutch
Paul Michael Glaser as Starsky

December 1971. It was cold in Boston that night. Then again, it is almost always cold in Boston every winter night. There was no snow on the ground, but the dirt outside my Beacon Hill brownstone was as hard as the sidewalk, and the little shrubs at the corner of Mt. Vernon and Charles Streets looked ready to pack it in for the rest of eternity.

As I crossed the Boston Commons, the trees looked darker, harder, of more substance as they curved tortuously toward the sky. The lake in the center of this Massachusetts park was frozen over and of a bluish, milky-white color, reflecting the light of the moon.

It was my first year of college, and I was on my way to the Cheri Theater to see the Norman Jewison film *Fiddler on the Roof*. At the time I was going to Emerson College, Henry Winkler's alma mater, and was preparing to start a new diet and rehearsals for the theater department's own production of *Fiddler*.

That was why I was trudging down Boylston Street by myself. The rest of my actor friends didn't want to bias their own performances, and the rest of my dormitory friends would rather see movies like *Kiss the Butt of my Gun* or something. So instead I arranged to meet my best friend, Steve, at the theater. Steve was majoring in theater at Boston University, which didn't do musicals when they could put on something nebulous and arty, so he wasn't worried about biasing anything. Especially since B.U. didn't let their new students act for the first two years anyway.

Soon I crossed through the Sheraton Hotel and arrived at the Cheri Theater, one, two, three. One, two, three, because they had built three long, small theaters with tiny screens instead of one wide theater with a huge screen. I was disappointed. What was the good of seeing a huge musical like *Fiddler* on a little screen? Why couldn't they put it in the Savoy or the Music Hall where it had a chance to be impressive (bear with me—all this has a point)?

Anyway, I met Steve, and we walked down to the first ten rows of seats and sat down on the aisle. We sat down on the aisle because I had just started Dr. Stillman's water diet, which called for six eight-ounce glasses of water a day in order to ''cleanse your system.'' I *had* to sit on the aisle in case my system needed cleansing twelve times during the movie. The Cheri had its air-conditioning on even in the middle of winter, so we kept our coats. Turns out that the interior

STARSKY AND HUTCH

Paul Michael Glaser

Born: March 25, 1943

Place of Birth: Cambridge, Massachusetts

Educated: Tulane University
　　　　　Boston University

Films: *Fiddler on the Roof* (with Topol)
　　　Butterflies are Free (with Edward
　　　　　Albert)
　　　Houdini: The Real Story (with
　　　　　Sally Struthers)

Plays: *The Man in the Glass Booth* (with
　　　　　Donald Pleasance)
　　　Butterflies are Free (with Keir Dullea)

Eyes: Hazel　Hair: Brown

Hobbies: Guitar, motorcycling, writing

David Soul

Born: August 28, 1943 (as David Solberg)

Place of Birth: Chicago, Illinois

Educated: Washington High School
　　　　　Colegio Americano
　　　　　University of Minnesota

Film: *Magnum Force* (with Clint Eastwood)

TV: *Here Come the Brides* (with Bobby
　　　Sherman

Eyes: Blue　Hair: Blond

Hobbies: Songwriting, baseball

chill helped us get into the mood of pre-World War I Russia.

The movie began. It was a full, golden, intelligent telling of the story of Tevya, a poor Russian milkman in the village of Anetevka. Tevya had five daughters, three of marrying age. He wanted them to wed rich, prosperous men who could make them comfortable. To Tevya, who was poor and married to a good-hearted shrew, comfort *was* happiness. But his girls wanted to marry for love, and therein lay the crux of the tale.

The background on which this tale unfolded was on a slightly larger scale. Tevya and his family were Jewish during a period of great Russian anti-Semitic persecution (so what else is new?). And brewing in Moscow was a great workers' revolution.

So, of course, it turns out that the youngest girl wants to marry a Russian soldier; the eldest wants to marry a poor Jewish tailor; and the middle girl wants to marry a penniless revolutionary named Perchik.

Perchik was played by a rugged-looking young man with dark, curly hair and a winning smile. All through the movie whenever I saw his face, I got the feeling that I knew him from somewhere (ever get that feeling?). Finally, during Perchik's final scene I leaned over to Steve.

"Who is that guy?"

"He's terrible."

"I know he's terrible. Who is he?"

"I could play that part with one hand tied behind my back."

"I know, I know. Doesn't he look familiar?" Steve looked closer, then leaned back into me. "Yeah."

"Who is he?"

"Hey, you two kids. Quiet there!"

"Who is he?," I whispered.

"Paul Michael Glaser."

"Who?" The name didn't ring any bells.

"Paul Michael Glaser. He went to B. U."

That's where I had seen him before. When I had first visited Boston University, I saw the same young man walking the hallways on the fourth floor of the School of Fine Arts. Yeah, Paul Michael Glaser.

Four years later I was in New York. I had been through two other universities besides Emerson and had lost eighty pounds before I finally got a job as an assistant editor of a comic-

David Soul as Hutch and Paul Michael Glaser as Starsky rap aboard their respective supercharged Fords.

book company. Only then did I discover, with the responsibility of twenty-one comic books and four magazines resting on my shoulders, that even after nearly fifteen years of education I was a semi-illiterate. After all, I had only been studying theater and cinema—what did I know about grammar and punctuation?

So I started writing professionally. I hunched over my notebooks, furiously scribbling for at least four hours a day, and came up with comic scripts, movie concepts, and several first chapters of novels. Occasionally I'd drop over to a friends' apartment on Twenty-third Street and read them what I had written. Besides, they had cable television, and, if my prose got boring, we could watch a movie.

One night the three of us were watching *I Love Lucy* and talking about California. I had not been on-stage for a year and was itching to try my luck in L.A.

"Don't," said Jodie, who was sitting in a tweed rocker near the phone. "I just talked to Dave, and he says it's miserable out there."

"That's nice," I said. "Who's Dave?"

"Dave Soul," she said. "He's a friend of mine."

"David Soul?," I said: "You mean the blond guy on *Here Come the Brides?*

"Yes."

"What?" said I. "He's working. I saw him on *Star Trek*. He plays one of the crooked cops in *Magnum Force*."

"Yeah?," said Jodie. "That's a big movie. He said he wasn't getting work."

"Sure," I drawled, the picture of intelligence. "He's working. What does he have to complain about?"

Such were my first meetings with Paul Michael Glaser and David Soul. My second meeting came about two years later after I had left the comic job (or it left me: it all depends on who you talk to), drifted back up to Boston, written a novel (it came out last October), and then returned to my home state of Connecticut, forty pounds heavier.

I sat down to watch an *A.B.C. Movie of the Week* that had looked good in the previews. The *Movie of the Week* at that time had that great opening with all those electric encircled ABCs coming at you like they did in the light-show segment of *2001: A Space Odyssey*. It was a per-

fect setup for whatever violent movie or domestic comedy the network had to offer.

But this time it was different. The movie that unfolded was a cop drama, to be sure, but with a difference. A difference that style made. The film seemed to be loosely based on the exploits of *The Super Cops,* a book and then a movie about two New York razzle-dazzle policemen nicknamed Batman and Robin. Only this network movie far outshone the theatrical one. These two cops were located in L.A.; they drove a red revved-up racing car with a nike-sneaker-like racing stripe along the side; and, man, they moved!

The Super Cops movie was muddled, cartoonish, and ineffective, but this A.B.C. television movie was meaty, layered, and fast, fast, fast. Everything about the plot, direction, photography, special effects, and acting seemed to be aimed at the audience's gut. These two super-cops didn't go around something when they could go *over* it. They didn't run down stairs; they careened. They didn't jump; they leaped.

One of them wore a baseball jacket, under which he carried a .357 magnum in a shoulder holster. A .357 magnum? Do you know how big a gun that is? You could look down the barrel of a .357 and see your whole life pass by in Cinerama!

The other guy wore a knitted fisherman's cap and either a bulky black-and-white sweater or an army jacket, under which he used an army .45 automatic. Whoo-boy. A slug from a .45 could hit Rosie Grier in the pinky and still floor him.

The plot, loosely told, began with the murder of two lovers in a car that looked just like the supercharged red one with the racing stripe. It seems that some professional hit men hit the wrong people by mistake. They were supposed to eliminate two cops named David Starsky and Ken Hutchinson, known to their compatriots and peers as Starsky and Hutch.

Once Starsky and Hutch learned of the failed murder attempt, they spent the rest of the picture trying to find out who wanted them dead and to eliminate the eliminators before they got eliminated themselves.

Among the flashy situations that they got themselves into were: getting caught in a cross-fire in an outdoor swimming pool in the middle of a torrential downpour, visiting an eccentric crime kingpin who was naked in his sauna except

Paul Michael as Dave Starsky, curly haired, leather jacketed, and intense.

for two towels and their shoulder-holstered guns, and an exciting climax that moved up and down several tens of flights of stairs in a hotel ablaze with gunfire.

Again, the one major difference between this cop show and all the others is that it had wit and a certain class, which was due to the costars, David Soul (I see he's working again) and Paul Michael Glaser (new and improved).

Besides the previously mentioned quality of production and a good script (in which Hutch was often called Starsky and Starsky Hutch until an aggravated Paul Michael exclaimed, "I'm Starsky; *he's* Hutch!") these two actors seemed born for their roles. There existed in them and between them a tension and a melding of style not seen since Paul Newman and Robert Redford hit the saddle for *Butch Cassidy and the Sundance Kid*.

David played the cool, capable Ken Hutchinson, a man of semiconservative tastes in clothes and cars as well as a health-food enthusiast, while Paul played Dave Starsky, the loose, moody, fast-food freak with exotic tastes and a car to match.

But it wasn't just the written characteristics that did the trick: it was what each of the young actors brought to the character. It was individual style and integrity that raised *Starsky and Hutch* from a good TV movie to a worldwide television-series smash.

DAVID SOUL

Ken Hutchinson's alter ego was born David Solberg on August 8, 1943 in Chicago, Illinois. His father was a college history professor as well as a Lutheran minister. David was already in a position to have strong opinions and to be forced to back them up. But he was hardly in a position to do so, since his family moved around constantly, what with his father being transferred from teaching job to teaching job and from parish to parish.

Finally, David managed to get some regularity into his life—but no normality. His father was appointed Religious Affairs Advisor to Germany by the State Department. Little David had to get used to a new country, a new language, new customs, and a whole new cultural situation.

Thankfully, the time spent abroad was an enriching experience. When the Solberg family returned to America, David was considering diplomacy as an occupation. But, as he entered the Washington High School in Sioux Falls, North Dakota to finish his preliminary education, other interests began to take hold.

His enthusiasm for sports and music occupied his thoughts after graduation, but perhaps he figured that neither of these was very secure as a profession. So David applied and was accepted to the Colegio Americano in Mexico City, majoring in political science.

But even there his musical and athletic talents held sway. The Chicago White Sox were interested in him as a ballplayer, but Dave thought it best to continue college and to develop his artistic skills. He went on to learn both the six- and the twelve-string guitar and from there got into a music society and played on Mexican television.

When Dave turned twenty, he transferred to the University of Minnesota. He was still majoring in political science, but he began to perform in clubs and coffeehouses to earn extra money. In order to better facilitate his personal, heartfelt career, Dave dropped the end of his name and added a u to become David Soul (a fitting pseudonym for a minister's son), which sounded a little more folksy.

That was also the year in which Dave got married for the first time. He and his wife had a son, Kris, soon after that and, unfortunately, a divorce a little while after that.

"We were both too young," David admitted.

Perhaps in order not to think about it, perhaps simply because it was what he had to do, Dave dove into his chosen career of singing. He worked his way to New York and, in order to continue developing his talent, started to take acting lessons. Then, in order to break through the multitude of mediocre singers, David created the persona of the Covered Man for himself, appearing in person with a ski mask to conceal his identity.

Even though it was sort of a cheap and somewhat demeaning ploy, it served its purpose. People began to notice him, and he appeared over twenty times on *The Merv Griffin Show* before he felt it was time to be "uncovered." A Screen Gems scout took note of the young, personable actor and signed him up. David Soul's acting career was off to a bumpy start.

And it basically stayed that way. He played

David Soul as Ken Hutchinson. Cool, easy-going, and dimpled.

supporting roles on *Flipper* and *I Dream of Jeannie* as well as appearing in "The Apple," an episode of the second season of *Star Trek*.

Even though he was working, the jobs weren't steady and the going was rough. David was smart enough to steadily keep trying to improve his ability by becoming a member of the Columbia Workshop, along with another young actor named Glaser.

Then it seemed as if David got the break that he needed to get his career going. He was cast in the semipopular series called *Here Come The Brides*. Semipopular because it was the most different show of the year. It concerned a logging town way up in the Seattle woods back in the early 1900s. The lumberjacks there were so lonely that a shipful of single ladies was brought over. And that was it.

The plot had everywhere and nowhere to go with a conception like that. And the same could be said for David. For he found himself playing third banana behind the strong-voiced Robert Brown and the nebulously talented Bobby Sherman. The latter played a stuttering youngster whom the public instantly took to heart. David Soul was lost amid the meandering story lines, the confused direction, and the furious idolatry of Bobby Sherman (who miraculously stopped stuttering in the second season).

Finally, *Here Come the Brides* died of an overdose of network confusion. No one seemed to know how to handle the program—as a drama, as a comedy, as an adventure, or what. So the show just sank, leaving David worse off than ever before.

Even though he had been given practically nothing to do on the show, the network saw him as typed. To them he was just another blond third banana, of which there were a multitude in Hollywood.

The horizon was not all black, however. Shortly after the show originally began, David fell in love and married one of his costars, Karen Carlson. Soon he had a second son to his name, Jon, but he also had the responsibility to feed him. So David got out his guitar and hit the road again.

Even though he managed to pick up an acting job here and there as well, things were not good. Finally, the rift in his professional and personal life widened, and he and Karen divorced.

Shortly after that bleak break he got another, a good one this time. *Dirty Harry,* the excellent and wildly successful Clint Eastwood movie about the character of San Francisco policeman Harry Callahan, was going into a sequel, and the producers cast David Soul as one of the villainous leads.

The movie was called *Magnum Force* after the gun Harry uses, a .44 magnum, the most powerful handgun ever made (Hutch's .357 is the second most powerful).

As Harry says in the film, "It can blow your head clean off."

The plot revolved around a team of three young, idealistic, attractive motorcycle cops, their leader played by Soul, who make it their business to illegally assassinate the criminal kingpins in their city.

In the rest of the movie Dirty Harry Callahan, who says, "It's all right to kill people if you kill the right people," gets involved with this group and then exterminates it. The violence and gore with which he does this were so extreme and so unremitting that I forgot whether David was drowned in the bay or had a precious portion of his anatomy blown off.

For, you see, the movie *Dirty Harry* was about a man. *Magnum Force* was about a gun. And there lies most of the difference. The rest of the difference lies in the fact that the first film was directed by Don Siegel, a master of the action genre, while *Magnum* was directed by, let us say, a pedestrian talent.

A pedestrian talent who seemed to think that the more gore you showed, the more gratuitous violence you put in, the better the film would be.

He was wrong. The film did well but basically catered to the sick side of our society. The critics were so repulsed that, whenever they did review the film, they rarely finished venting their spleen in time to see some of its good qualities. Such as a good script by Michael Cimino (*Thunderbolt and Lightfoot*) and John Milius (*The Wind and the Lion*), admirable performances by Clint and Hal Holbrook, and the magnetism of a certain David Soul.

Which brings us up to 1975. *Magnum* didn't seem to help David's career beyond the original exposure and money. He was still scraping by and developing in the Screen Gems Training Program for actors when he read for producer

Clint Eastwood (left) as Harry Callahan and Hal Holbrook (second standing from right) give David Soul's big 357 a second look in the violent opus, "Magnum Force."

Aaron Spelling and again met another young man named Glaser.

PAUL MICHAEL GLASER

The man with the warm hazel eyes, curly brown hair, and curled, cocksure smile always seems to come on strong as Dave Starsky. He is always giving the impression of a secure, intelligent, adjusted individual. Well, there's a good reason for this. He is.

Paul was born March 25, 1943 in Cambridge, Massachusettes. Cambridge, right across the Charles River from Boston, is part of one of the most lovely city areas in the country. Trees are not precious commodities, as in New York, and a beautiful river view is about a twenty-minute walk from anywhere, while a beautiful natural view is about a twenty-minute drive.

The Boston area thrives with education: there are over two hundred colleges, with M.I.T. and Harvard, two of the best educational establishments anywhere, in Cambridge. The streets are always filled (not too full) with students, and the bookstores, clothes stores, record shops, restaurants, and coffeehouses are always alive with conversation and activity.

This was the environment in which the young Glaser was shaped. His father was a successful architect and his mother worked at home, so Paul never really wanted for comfort. One of Paul's two older sisters was interested in acting and shared her experiences with him. Then much more than now, though, anybody who was interested in theater was laughed at at worst or thought a sissy at best by his peers (as were John Travolta, Gabe Kaplan, and Henry Winkler), so Paul protected himself by becoming the best athlete he could. All through his school years, though, he concentrated on developing his inner resources as well.

As a result the young man was somewhat withdrawn, inner-directed, and intense when he graduated. Instead of following roads suggested to him by the actions of his peers or society Paul followed his dream. Acting.

"When I was growing up," Paul said, "I would watch films and go 'gee whiz' at people in the movies."

But he followed his dream constructively by getting accepted to Tulane University in New Orleans, majoring in theater and English and minoring in architecture (never hurts to have a backup occupation, y'know).

Whereas many other prospective acting hopefuls would rush off to New York and L.A. to try their luck, Paul's life is marked by his more intelligent conviction. Instead of putting himself in an all-or-nothing situation right away he seemed to go in a direction suitable to a gradual control of his art.

For instance, after graduating from Tulane he didn't leap pell-mell into the acting profession: he went to get his master's at Boston University instead. And after that he didn't rush right out to the acting capitals of the country: he chose to sharpen his skills with five years of repertory and summer-stock work.

Only then did he seem to feel that he was ready to enter the clawing camaraderie that marked the New York theater scene. There Paul was lucky and talented enough to get to work with Joseph Papp, one of New York's greatest play producers. Mr. Papp believes in developing the inherent ability of any good actor as well as the sanctity of the theater. Look at any groundbreaking, modern, controversial, successful show on or around Broadway, and you'll probably see Joseph Papp's name as producer.

Paul performed in a rock version of *Hamlet* for Papp, which led to several off-Broadway roles. Paul's first notices were due to his appearance in two Broadway successes almost back to back.

The Man in the Glass Booth, written by Robert Shaw (*Jaws, The Deep*), who also wrote *A Man for All Seasons*, was the first. It was an electrifying play about the subject of Naziism and showcased an award-winning performance by Donald Pleasance.

Butterflies are Free was the second, in which Paul played the fourth of an unfortunately basically three-person play. It was the story of a blind man, based on lawyer Hal Krentz, who was trying to escape the apronstrings of his clinging, overprotective mother by living with the girl next door. Paul was not the blind man, the mother, the girl, or the apron strings. But the show was a good credit (he was the girl next door's ex-boyfriend).

Following that Paul started to make the soap-opera rounds. His first assignment was a six-month stint as a psychiatrist on *Love is a Many-*

Starsky and Hutch, circa first season.
Notice Starsky's short hair and wool cap.

splendored Thing. He was in good company there. *Love's* cast included David Groh (*Rhoda*), Andrea Marcovicci (*The Front*), and David Birney (*Serpico*).

Then came nine months on *Love of Life* as Dr. Joe Corelli, who first treated Bill Prentiss for leukocytemia and then tried desperately to secure evidence to clear Tess Prentiss from a charge of first-degree murder after Bobby Mackey was found dead. (To better understand this confusing mystery, see *The Illustrated Soap Opera Companion*, also by yours truly, also from Drake Publishers.) Needless to say, Paul was kept hopping.

An interesting sidelight. At that time Paul went by the name of Michael Glaser, for it seemed that there was another Paul Glaser, on the Actor's Equity rolls. Only when the other Paul Glaser passed away did Paul Michael resume the use of his full name. Isn't that interesting?

Well, back to organized biography. Paul was smart enough to leave the soaps before he made too great an impression. Paul has the reputation of being a stickler for detail, so that and probably his intention not to get typed as a soap actor led to his moving to California. Once he was settled there, it seems as if he got the Perchik role in *Fiddler* almost right away.

Which brings us back to our first meeting. I'm sorry to say that Paul did not make a very good impression on me (as if he should care) in the movie. He played Perchik with a strident conviction, settling for a two-dimensional reading of, granted, a two-dimensional part. Paul Michael's Perchik was a revolutionary with the body of a twenty-year-old, the manner of a teenager, and the motivations of a child (how much of this was to blame on the director is unknown to me).

Beyond my disappointment the professional critics rarely deemed to mention Glaser at all. Instead they either seemed to blanketly pan or praise the movie, ignoring individual contributions. Suffice it to say that Paul Michael's movie debut was a mixed blessing. It gave him a top-notch credit, but it didn't set the casting agents ablaze.

Paul kept going, and his career chugged along. He too got involved in the guest-star racket, sowing his acting oats on *Kojak, The Waltons, The Streets of San Francisco, Toma,* and *The Rockford Files.* Then came the opportunity to audition for Starsky. Paul was chosen almost immediately out of eighty possibilities because, as one insider puts it: "Paul *is* Dave Starsky. He was exactly what we were looking for."

Says Paul: "I've been waiting all my life to play Starsky."

Watching him every week, that statement can readily be believed.

DAVID HUTCH—KEN SOUL—PAUL MICHAEL STARSKY—DAVE GLASER

The roles indeed look tailor-made for these two talented young men. It was their strength as people and as actors that turned this cop show into something special. Different? Yes. Effective? Definitely. Controversial? You bet! Whether in the long run the show is considered helpful or harmful in relation to the violent context of almost all the modern arts is practically beside the point. It is, no matter what you think about its content, a good show. So good, as a matter of fact, that it is not only a big hit here but the number-one show in England and the only American program ever to win the British Emmy.

My attitude, my opinion, my theory is that *Starsky and Hutch* is not only worthwhile and entertaining but important as well. For many reasons, good and bad.

(1) It is straight, well-made fantasy. No real cops could do, let alone get away with, the spectacular things that Starsky and Hutch manage to achieve. Maybe once or twice in a lifetime but not every week.

Their world of mad driving, spectacular stunts, far-out predicaments and locations, huge, powerful, booming guns, and stylized fights approaching slapstick is made not to be taken seriously. Throughout history fantasy has been made violent and exciting. From the Brothers Grimm to Shakespeare to *The Lord of the Rings.* It in itself should not be harmful. It is only when reality is packaged as fantasy or made to seem like fantasy, as on the network news and the media outlets, that fantasy becomes dangerous.

(2) Soul and Glaser have, largely through their own best efforts, created caring, concerned, mul-

Starsky and Hutch, second season.
Same sweaters, but, man, dig the crazy change.

Off stage.

tilayered human beings out of the characters of Starsky and Hutch. Grown men not afraid to express themselves or feel the hard emotions.

Each one allows himself moods and the ability to go through changes. There are times on the show when Starsky and Hutch hug. They aren't afraid of contact. Their masculinity is never in doubt. There are times when each of them has cried. It is not something that they have tried to hide or suppress. Again, it didn't make them any less masculine. It made them more human.

(3) The show *Starsky and Hutch* has developed a sense of the victim. During their first season, even though the program had a certain sort of seamy sensitivity, their victims, like every other victim on TV cop shows, were just that. Victims. People who were raped, murdered, or mutilated in the first five minutes of the show and hardly ever mentioned again. The other fifty minutes were taken up with the "good guys" tracking down the "bad guys" and bringing them to "justice" (whether it be to the precinct house or to the cemetery). But what for? What's these cops' motivation besides "doing their jobs?"

Well, it seems that Glaser and Soul saw this gaping fallacy in the action series. It was all the difference between drama and a body count. So they took steps to correct it. During the second season a common plot line would involve Starsky and Hutch with someone who's threatened with rape, murder, or mutilation, and in the rest of the program we could get to know that person and maybe begin to care. By the time the danger to the victim became imminent, we would be all the more relieved when Hutch and Starsky (change of pace) came thundering to the rescue. They had saved a person, not just a mindless, faceless number or thing.

Of course, every show is not exactly like this, and the two men didn't achieve these changes alone. The writers, directors, and, most important, their producer, Aaron Spelling, go along with the guys. He knows that they want to make the show the best and so does he. For some reason the bond of trust that Glaser and Soul share has spread out to affect almost everyone involved with the making of the show. (Aaron Spelling is a fascinating combination of genius and schlockmaster whom we'll get into later.)

Nowhere, however, is that bond stronger than between the two young actors themselves. Even with all their physical and mental differences they have become like brothers.

And they have branched out. On Halloween night, 1976 Paul Michael appeared magically on an A.B.C. television movie as the greatest of all illusionists, Harry Houdini. He's come a long way since Perchik.

David Soul has two TV movies shuffling for air time at this writing. He also has an album mostly of original songs.

Evidence of their fame is everywhere. It has been a long time in coming, and by all the evidence of the two men's lives and goals they are well worth it.

Robert Blake as "Baretta."

BARETTA

(don't do the act if you don't have the past, don't do it)

Robert Blake as Baretta

Robert Blake is the meanest little bugger on television. He's also one of the best actors on television. Even though he may be just going through the motions occasionally on *Baretta*, he's still one of the best actors anywhere. Because he's got the equipment. He's got the love and the hate inside him, ready to give.

Television is a thankless, thankless medium. First, the creator has no audience other than the ratings, and the ratings are a representative poll of only a percentage of the population. And a small percentage at that. So how does the creator know who's applauding and who's turning him off?

Second, even if you have a hit show, week after week all you know are lights and stage crews and scripts and cameras. There's no give-and-take between you, the creator, and they, the audience. For you it's always give, give, give day after day, month after month, year in, year out. For them, for *us*, the audience, it's take, take, take, and then, when we get tired, we just switch channels. And then there are the middlemen. The little network employees whose job it is to keep the status quo. To make sure that it stays the way it is.

Sure, they pay the creator lots of money and

from time to time give him an award and lots of personal appearances. But the money can run out tomorrow; the awards are for what you do, not who you are; and the people come out to meet your character, the part you play, not you.

So what do you do? You do your job. Then you either take steps to protect yourself or get out. Once you're in the business, it's not what you can do but who you are that dictates whether you get out alive.

For a long time Robert Blake didn't know who he was. For a long time. Now *we* know who he is. He's Anthony Baretta, the Italian supercop who cares more for the people on his beat than for the restrictions of his job. Given that definition, I might as well be describing Robert Blake.

Morning in L.A. With the limos and Continentals and Cadillacs and Rolls Royces on Mulholland Drive and the rest of the Hollywood roadways leading to Mecca, the studios, the air is already tight with pollutants. Nobody seems to walk in this town. The palm trees wave at the concrete sidewalks as soundstages all over start revving up for their daily tasks.

Thousands upon thousands of skilled and unskilled technical laborers start checking over

71

BARETTA

Robert Blake

Born: September 13, 1939

Place of Birth: Nutley, New Jersey

Nationality: Italian

Educated: Too numerous to mention

Films: *Our Gang*
     Red Ryder
     Treasure of Sierra Madre (with
        Humphrey Bogart)
     Harmony (with John Garfield)
     Pork Chop Hill (with Gregory Peck)
     P.T. 109 (with Cliff Robertson)
     The Greatest Story Ever Told
        (with Max Von Sydow)
     This Property is Condemned
        (with Charles Bronson)
     In Cold Blood
     Tell Them Willie Boy is Here
        (with Robert Redford)
     Corky
     Busting (with Elliot Gould)
     Electra Glide in Blue

Height: 5' 9"

Eyes: Brown

Hair: Black

Hobbies: Motorcycles

Address: c/o ABC
        4151 Prospect Ave.
        Hollywood, Cal. 90027

their scripts and charts, stepping over electrical cords, and setting up equipment. These men have long ago stopped being in awe of stars. Now they respect stars only in relation to how much time they save them. The crew sets to its respective tasks. For every two minutes of adventure that you see on the screen, there are two hours of meticulous camera-, light-, and soundwork. For two minutes of action there may have been two days of razzle-dazzle technical ploys.

The *Baretta* soundstages are technically no different. Physically, there's a big difference. About five feet nine of pure packed power. A mercurial whiz who walks on the set and, just by being himself, controls everyone. The man with as much respect for his troops as they have for him. You know who I'm talking about, don't you?

Robert Blake was born, trapped, in a poor section of Nutley, New Jersey on September 13, 1939 as Robert Gubitosi. He was trapped with a brother and a sister. His father was a show nut.

Blake has said: "He'd sit around all day long and play Caruso records and sing along . . . It was a crazy house."

But at another time he admitted: "He was a monster. Alone with his . . . craziness and total paranoia . . . he'd get up in the middle of the night . . . come in, and beat the crap out of us."

Robert's career started when he was two years old. His father got up a song-and-dance act, which he made the boy perform on weekends. Then he was pushed on stage as one of the Three Little Hillbillies, another parental brainstorm. Robert wasn't happy but he didn't mind, because it "kept me away from home." But his parent-inflicted career was just getting started.

Chasing down the dollar signs, Robert was brought to the West Coast, where the precocious child was cast as Mickey in the M.G.M. *Our Gang* comedies. He shared a studio with the likes of Spencer Tracy, Gene Kelly, and Judy Garland but shared a life with experiences not worthy of anybody.

" . . . Forcing a kid to be a performer is one of the worst things that can happen to a child," he says now.

Especially when there is no communication between family members. His mother was trapped in the rut of life as well. She wasn't close to

*Then and now. Robert Blake as Perry King in his fabulous,
but generally overlooked, performance in "In Cold Blood."*

her husband; she wasn't close to her children, whom she had created from her very being. The Gubitosis were trapped in the hell of tinsel and bright-lighted fantasies. With no letup. At ten Robert was signed as Little Beaver, the Indian sidekick of Wild Bill Elliot in the *Red Ryder* series.

"Being a kid takes time," Robert says, and he was robbed. On talk shows you might have heard his stories about how his mother kept putting him up on the horses when he didn't understand and was afraid of them. But little Robert was the Gubitosi's bread and butter, so on the horses he would stay for as long as they could make him. Robert did as he was told.

After the Western series died, Robert traded his Indian makeup for Mexican makeup, playing opposite the legendary Humphrey Bogart as Fred C. Dobbs in *The Treasure of Sierra Madre*. From there he played other roles in other movies, the highlight of which was *Harmony*, starring the great though largely forgotten John Garfield. Garfield was short and tough, with the same sort of wide, sensitive face that Blake has. And his film roles matched his countenance. Backstage as well he was gentle and kind, and Robert will probably never forget him. Blake's past is part and parcel of the present man.

Finally, Robert was old enough to rebel. All his life he had wanted love, and all he got was patient reactions or downright aggression. Blake needed warmth, but everything he touched seemed cold and artificial. So he fought against the only thing left. Himself.

Because his parents always seemed to see him only as a threat or as a commodity, Robert got down on everybody. He thought people were garbage. On Hollywood soundstages there wasn't anyone who would go out of his way to prove otherwise, so people, to Robert, became crap. And, if people were crap, then the world was crap. And, if the world was crap, then he was crap. And, if he was crap, it didn't make any difference what happened to him.

Through the rest of his young life Robert struggled very hard to prove that everything was lousy. When he was fourteen, he left home. But the outside world proved harsher even than his own house. He came back to try again, but things were even worse. His acting career had died of neglect. Robert continued to fight the teachers

and his fellow students at any school that would have him.

"I was Los Angeles' first assigned-risk high-school student," he jokes now.

But then it was no joke. Then no one could handle him. Most didn't want to, and the rest didn't try. Robert was shuttled around five high schools in two years. He messed around with booze; he had constant run-ins with the law and the vice squad. Even in a crowd he was alone.

Finally, it was all too much. The city was closing in on him. Simply to get away, Blake joined the army. He was assigned to a base in Alaska, where he found a new kind of escape. Drugs.

"For years people always let me down. I thought people were no good," Robert said in an article, "...so...I'd stick a lousy needle in my arm."

Soon that escape became even more horrible than the reality that he ran from. Because it was temporary. The escape was false. It didn't help things: it only made them worse when he came down. Robert traded it in for the pursuit of himself. Whatever it must have been like—coming to the decision, going through cold turkey to beat his addiction, and living the big change—only Robert knows. And he's not talking. He's not about to relive it for reporters or writers. Suffice it to say that he discovered that someone did care, that he was important, and that life was not something you wished it to be but something you made.

Robert figured that it was worth trying to live instead of finding ways to die. He got out of the army; he got married to a strong, loving woman; and he went back to the only thing that he ever really wanted to do, acting.

As you know, Robert's story has a happy ending. But it didn't happen overnight and it wasn't easy. It was a hard, upward struggle, but after twenty-five years he got there.

1959: *Pork Chop Hill,* Director Lewis Milestone's brutal and effective commentary on the futility of war. Robert Blake played one of the valiant soldiers under the command of Gregory Peck who were ordered to take and hold a meaningless hunk of land during the Korean War only to save face for the United States' representatives at the peace talks less than seventy miles away.

Now, Robert is making it big as Baretta. His role as the super cop has garnered an Emmy, as well as many other awards.

1951: *Town Without Pity*. Robert Blake played Jim, the most disturbed of the four G.I.s who raped a German girl while they were stationed there. Defense Attorney Kirk Douglas got the four off, but the humiliated girl committed suicide. Anything but a popular classic.

1963: *P.T. 109*. Robert Blake played Bucky Harris to Cliff Robertson's John F. Kennedy in the more-or-less-straight retelling of Kennedy's exploits in the Second World War.

1965: *The Greatest Story Ever Told*. Robert Blake played Simon the Zealot in a grand retelling of the story of Christ.

1965: *Harry, Noon and Night*. A change of place but not of theme. Bobby was on Broadway in the leading role of Harry in a play that ran a total of six performances. As usual, it was a harsh story with overtones of mental cruelty and homosexuality. The *New York Times* described Blake as "angry, persistent, mocking . . . foaming and fury . . . becomes excessive, then downright maniacal."

1966: *This Property is Condemned*. Blake joined Charles Bronson, Robert Redford, and Natalie Wood in this grimy tale of southern morality. Another angry, unsavory outing.

Then in 1967 came the most unsavory of all. Robert Blake, even after all his years in the business, was cast, largely because he was an excellent "unknown," as Perry Smith in Richard Brook's production of Truman Capote's book *In Cold Blood*.

At 2:00 A.M. on the night of November 15, 1959 the four members of the Herbert Clutter family were murdered for what turned out to be forty-three cents. Brooks' movie followed the real life-and-death story of Perry Smith and Dick Hickock—why they did the crime and how they were caught. The film, based on fact, is destined to be a classic of its kind and is still powerful today, even on television.

After seeing it originally I hoped and fully expected Robert Blake's performance to win an Oscar and start him on a hugely successful career. He wasn't even nominated. The film was so realistically filmed and the studio counted so much on its realism to draw audiences that the fact that professional actors were playing the roles was skirted over, played down, or ignored. Robert did an excellent job, one that he is still proud of today, but, as far as his career was con-

cerned, he was back to square one. If not a half a step back. It was almost two years before his next film was released.

1969: *Tell Them Willie Boy Is Here*. Blake was back in the saddle. Sort of. Director Sydney Pollack (*They Shoot Horses, Don't They?*, *Jeremiah Johnson*, *The Way We Were*, *Three Days of the Condor*) was starting his creative partnership with Robert Redford at this time. Redford played Christopher Cooper, known as Coop, a sheriff in an Indian-reservation town shortly after the turn of the twentieth century. Robert Blake played the title role, a Paiute Indian who returned to his home, the reservation, taking up where he had left off with his love, Lola (played by Katherine Ross).

Only Lola's brothers and father frowned on the relationship. And one night they tried to forcibly show Willie Boy the error of his ways. In the ensuing fight Willie accidentally kills Lola's father. The rest of the film consists of Willie Boy's escape with Lola into the Mojave Desert and Coop's reluctant manhunt.

Again, the tone and theme of the film are bleak and show the darker side of human experience. Coop's posse is bigoted and bloodthirsty; the frail Lola dies of exposure; and in the end Willie Boy forces Coop to kill him when he points a gun that he knows isn't loaded at the sheriff.

Blake's performance was exceptional, as usual, full of bite and ivory, but again, the audiences and critics weren't responding. Blake continued to struggle into the seventies. With his career and himself. Throughout the period when he was making his "comeback," Blake had been in professional therapy, trying to get a line on his life.

He was still making his way when ultraviolence hit the movie screens. Sam Peckinpah started it all with *The Wild Bunch*, a bloodily detailed account of the end of the famous Hole in the Wall gang (another more popular version was made by George Roy Hill, entitled *Butch Cassidy and the Sundance Kid*). After the same director's *Straw Dogs* a steady stream of gory, gratuitous, sensationalistic adventures glutted the movie market.

Bob Blake wasn't immune to appearing in productions of this kind. He starred in the rarely seen *Corky*, about a down-and-out racecar driver, as well as the scarcely more prestigious *Busting* with Elliot Gould.

*Robert's performance as a feisty motorcycle cop in "Electra Glide in Blue,"
was supposed to send him into the superstar realm. It went nowhere.*

Busting was another mangy little movie about the dark side of life. Its bleakness was derived not only from its subject matter but also from the photography: almost the entire project was shot in such a way that the color was a washed-out yellow.

Blake played, according to *Time* magazine, "[a] good, dogged street cop who knows where the action is [sounds like a certain I-talian wonder, don't it?]." Along with his partner he rebels against the restrictions of the police department in order to nail a big-time drug pusher. In the script the two intrepid policemen go through houses of prostitution, savage beatings, junkies, waltzing in gay bars, and a crazy chase-shootout in ambulances.

Time magazine called the film itself "adept and forceful . . . deriving its energy . . . from the skill of its . . . stars."

Still, the quality-role offers didn't come pouring in.

The third of Blake's four "big breaks" came when United Artists decided to gamble on one James Guercio, who until then was a rock producer of such stars as Chicago and Blood, Sweat, and Tears. Guercio had a movie script called *Electra Glide in Blue*, which U.A. bet would be the surprise smash of 1973. They gave the young producer-director carte blanche and instigated a publicity campaign rivaling that of *King Kong*.

Guercio's film concerned a short, feisty motorcycle cop by the name of Jim Wintergreen, who was in search of a promotion to detective through his own department's corruption and the bleakness of the human soul. Guercio cast Robert Blake as Wintergreen.

Time called his performance "blunt and high-charged."

Newsweek said that Wintergreen was deftly played by Blake.

They weren't as nice to the film itself. *Electra Glide in Blue* was too derivative and pretentious, they said. Guercio's self-admitted "answer to *Easy Rider*" died at the box office, and Robert's career breakthrough never happened.

But his private breakthrough did. Through the wise handling of the situation by a skilled psychiatrist Robert discovered that: "the demands I was making were too big . . . for the world. And that the world was not at fault. I was

looking for that kind of love . . . you can only get from parents."

It was no wonder that the rest of the world always seemed to fail him. He was looking for something that he had to find in himself first.

Robert Blake took a long, hard look at himself. His movie career was going nowhere. He had a wife whom he loved deeply and two kids for whom he wanted only the best. He had decided when little Noah and Dellnah were born that he and his wife Sondra would give them the home that he never had. Give them the love, the dedication, and the respect that he never got and that only a parent could give. So Sondra gave up her career as an actress and dancer for awhile. Robert accepted no location work, and they raised their two children. He had to make some kind of decision. How was he going to keep the family fed without taking the kind of parts that he usually did and was known for?

The answer came quickly. Roy Huggins had another hit cop show on the air about a real-live cop named Dave Toma. Tony Musante was playing the role of the unorthodox undercover investigator who relied on stealth and disguises more than on violence and gunplay. But after only one season Musante left simply to avoid being typed as either Toma or as a television star. The network was left with a hit conception but no star! Where would they find another versatile Italian with the personality to save *Toma?*

In Robert Blake, that's where. Even though his agent told him that he was crazy to take up an already established series in midseason, Blake grabbed the opportunity to do his thing with a full deck. The basic concept of a "cop with a thousand faces" was kept, but Robert brought his own brand of machismo and integrity to the role. His character was named after a gun known to be small but effective. *Baretta*!

The audience began noticing changes immediately. Whereas Toma was married to a beautiful girl and lived in a nice little house, Baretta lived in the cellar of a rundown hotel run by an old, eccentric drunk who lived with a cockatoo named Fred. Whereas Toma was reluctant to use force, Baretta wouldn't hesitate to use the language and methods of the jungle. He treated scum like scum. Whereas Toma was

Now when he hits the street on his bike, everybody knows him.

*Baretta does his thing with the help of Billy as played by Tom Ewell (left)
and Fred the Cockatoo.*

tough but diplomatic, Baretta was tougher and always told it like it was. For the audience every change was for the better. *Baretta* took over and surpassed the popularity of *Toma*.

And you better believe that it was practically all Robert Blake's doing. The show really began to catch on after his Emmy award as Best Actor and repeated guest shots on *The Tonight Show*. With Johnny Carson Blake let it all hang out, becoming the most talked-about guest since Jackie Onassis. People got to know the unique man behind *Baretta* on *The Tonight Show* as well as delighting in his wit, his integrity, and his unusual usage of the English language. And you can take dat to the bank!

Baretta soon became an extension of the Blake persona. Honest, gutsy, caring. The crew was dedicated to the man, and soon the feisty little devil was in control of almost the entire production of *Baretta*.

To ensure the continued quality of the program, Blake went "to the mat," as he puts it, with the network execs. Shortly after the first season he wanted certain guarantees, certain things understood, and certain qualifications met. First he threatened to quit, then he want to court to ensure these things.

"I had fights last season," said Robert. "I'll have fights next season. It's the only way to make my point with the producers."

Robert Blake got his demands. *Baretta* is run by, to, and for him. The level of quality remains high, and it is Blake's work that is responsible. He stays on the set an average of ten hours a day; he supervises everything; and nothing, but nothing, eludes his participation or consideration. Since no one else seems to care, Robert figures that it's his ass and he had better care.

"In television," he said in an article, "their theory is to put the money in the pot. Once it's on the air, forget about it, screw it."

Elsewhere in the same article he says: "I

spend all my time working on this . . . trying to bring lousy scripts to life, trying to bring mannequins with suits on to life. On the show I work off a lot of hate."

He works off a lot of love, too. Robert is generous to a fault and kind to those, as they say, less fortunate than himself. His work for charities is frequent and extensive. But it goes beyond that. If you have watched the program this season, you may have noticed a semiregular man playing a black cop with hoarse voice named Fats. Robert Blake found the man on-location one day. He was a drunk, a bum, a derelict. Robert cleaned him up and got him a part on the show but with a promise to stay sober during working hours. Otherwise no strings attached. That shows just a little of the depth of Blake's concern and conviction.

Robert Blake knows where he's going. He knows where he's been, and he never intends to visit that neck of the woods again. He hasn't seen his mother in ten years. His father died in 1955. He doesn't see his brother or sister. But his wife is back to work, and his kids are growing up right. The secret, Bob says, is not to teach them but to learn from them.

Sondra has guested on *Baretta* twice as well as costarring in *The Killer Elite* (with James Caan, Bob Hopkins, and Burt Young), *Helter Skelter*, and *Bound for Glory*. Her performances in all of them have been effective and riveting.

And Bob has stopped running. He's still moving and working, but he's not afraid of himself anymore. The bitterness, the hate is all constructively directed now.

"The thing I learned is this," says Robert Blake, "I am what I am. For most of my life I tried to put that away and be like other people. But . . . if you can take that . . . that whatever is in you and . . . find a way to make that work, then you'll be O.K."

You're O.K., Robert Blake. Amen.

Lee Majors as Steve Austin, "The Six Million Dollar Man."

THE SIX MILLION DOLLAR MAN
AND THE BIONIC WOMAN

(the big bionic boondoggle, or the cosmic-comic cyborg caper)

Lee Majors as The Six Million Dollar Man
Lindsay Wagner as the Bionic Woman
Richard Anderson as Oscar Goldman

For every generation it's different. Last generation it was pulp magazines and radio. For my generation it was television and comic books. This generation it's science fiction and movies. But no matter what it is and no matter what its true effect is, to parents it's all the same. It rots your brain.

As my father read of and listened to the golden exploits of *The Spider, Operator #5, The Shadow, Doc Savage, Racket Squad, Lights Out, Space Cadet,* and *Dragnet,* his parents would say, "Don't listen to that stuff—it'll rot your brain."

As I read the fabulous adventures of *The Fantastic Four, Daredevil, The Silver Surfer, The Hulk,* and *Spider-Man,* my mother would say: "Why do you buy that stuff? It rots your brain."

And now, as my young friends lap up *The Destroyer* paperbacks, as they run to see the exploits of James Bond and Dirty Harry, and as they watch the daring doings of *The Six Million Dollar Man* and *The Bionic Woman,* I say nothing. I just read along, run along, and watch along with them!

I know what we are doing. I realize the good in it. We are doing the same thing that I used to do with *Tarzan, Flash Gordon, The Man from*

U.N.C.L.E., Secret Agent, The Prisoner, The Planet of the Apes, and many others. We are finding heroes. And we are releasing our tensions through fantasy.

Today it is more important than ever. In the seventies the grip of apathy and the almost visible fear hanging over our everyday lives are stronger than they have been since the fifties, McCarthyism, Communism, and the atom bomb. Today it's Watergate, street violence, and corruption. In the fifties it was simple. We had the government and the police to take care of us. But today the government and the police can't be trusted. They are human just like the rest of us and have proven fallible again and again.

So who can the youth turn to? Who has the conviction, the intelligence, and the *power* to win out over all evil? The bionic duo, that's who. This guy and gal who not only have super-powered, artifical areas of their anatomy but are vulnerable, sensitive, and good-looking as well.

Harve Bennett, the executive producer of both bionic shows, said it best in an article: ". . . in this era of public scandal and cynicism, I felt the time was right for an old-fashioned, idealistic hero . . . who comes along to fight evil."

But Harve was smart. He was a TV man who

83

BIONIC BUDDIES

Lee Majors

Born: No exact date — orphan

Real Name: Harvey Lee Yeary

Place of Birth: Wyandotte, Michigan

Films: *Will Penny* (with Charlton Heston)
The Liberation of L.B. Jones (with
Anthony Zerbe)
The Francis Gary Powers Story

Height: 6' 1"   Weight: 185 pounds

Eyes: Blue   Hair: Brown   Hobbies: Hunting

———

Lindsay Wagner

Born: June 22, 1949

Place of Birth: Los Angeles, California

Parents: Bill Wagner and Marilyn Thrasher

Educated: University of Oregon
Mt. Hood Community College

Films: *Two People* (with Peter Fonda)
The Paper Chase (with Timothy Bottoms)

Height: 5' 9"   Hair: Tawny blond

Eyes: Olive   Hobbies: Singing

Address: c/o ABC
4151 Prospect Ave.
Los Angeles, Cal. 90027

knew that, if his characters were superhuman or caricatured, they wouldn't be very interesting after a few weeks, so ". . . he had to be questioning . . . and in jeopardy every so often."

BIONIC BIRTH

Heroic fantasy has never had an easy time of it on TV. By television's very nature it is designed to be an inexpensive medium where, more than anywhere else, time is money. Often, even if one would like to lavish time and money on a certain project, since the show has to be on week to week, it is impossible. Even though the basic idea may be of cosmic proportions, the universes have to be trimmed, the characters have to be cut down, and the grandiose heroics kept to a minimum.

TV's earliest attempts were, even by the day's standards, pretty laughable. *Captain Video* and *Tom Corbutt, Space Cadet* were cheap studio productions, and even series of the *Lone Ranger* and especially *Superman* couldn't fully extend their themes.

All were locked into pretty much pedestrian accomplishments because of the limitations of the television format. Anything expensive or time-consuming was frowned upon. So complicated special effects weren't considered, and mind-blowing, monumental situations were simply yearned for. (Imagine if they had ever had Superman take on an army or push over a skyscraper!)

These constrictions have extended even into today. Even though advanced technology and inflation have opened up possibilities somewhat, almost every show is still prevented in some way from realizing its fantastic potential.

Star Trek was constantly berated by its own network. *Batman,* instead of being presented as the atmospheric, powerful detective that he was in the comics, was formed into a potbellied, camp fool. *Space: 1999,* even with its tremendous special effects, is nullified by moronic writing that surpasses understanding. And continually horror and science-fiction anthology series are put up against rating kings in a seemingly serious attempt to bury them, as in the cases of *The Outer Limits, Tales of the Unknown,* and this season's *Tales of The Unexpected.*

Understandably enough, studio executives,

In action, at sixty miles per hour (slow motion, of course).

who most often are educated along the lines of moronic situation comedies, lookalike dramas, and game shows, don't understand the fantastic, the different, or the supernatural. As soon as they are presented with it, they seem to react by trying to normalize it, cut it down, and water it up to make it "acceptable," at the same time effectively causing it to lose its attractability. That was why *The Outer Limits* had to have "a monster a week." That was why *Star Trek* had to have a "galactic threat a week." That was why *Batman* had to remain as moronic as it was, even though its pitiful concept was what led it to an early grave.

But a book called *Cyborg* by Martin Caidin came to the attention of Harve Bennett. It was about a man named Steve Austin who was rebuilt by the government after a terrible plane accident, using the science of bionics, and thereby became a cyborg.

Bionics is biology as applied to electronic-engineering systems. A cyborg is a *cyb*ernetic *org*anism. Cybernetics is the science of computers in relation to the human nervous system. Did you get all that? Well, basically, Steve Austin's destroyed limbs were replaced by artificial electronic limbs, attached to his own nerves and controlled by his own brain! He became not quite a man, not quite a robot.

Bennett was fascinated by the possibilities of the novel as a television pilot. Not only did it have the conflict of the androidized Austin vs. the enemies of the U.S. but also the inherent conflict of man against machine to dwell on.

So Caidin was paid, a conception was okayed, a script was written, and a ninety-minute movie planned. And who did Bennett cast as Steve Austin, the semihuman who cost the government six million dollars to recreate? C'mon, all together now! *Lee Majors!*

Bennett needed a physical presence to match the as yet undreamed-of superfeats of the bionic man. He found just that in the physique and experience of Lee Majors. Majors has a muscular body best described as "beefy." He's big but not too big. He's muscular but not musclebound. With his straight, dark hair, narrow, piercing eyes, strong, pointed nose, and thin lips, Majors represented just the right combination of human and hero. Lee's past added to his ability to play a flawed superman.

BIONIC BIOGRAPHY

At the tender age of thirteen the young Lee, born Harvey Lee Yeary in Wyandotte, Michigan, discovered by accident that he was an adopted orphan. He was exploring in the attic of his home when he came across some newspaper articles stating that his real mother had been killed in a car accident when he was two and that his real father had died in a steel-mill accident before he was born!

But instead of feeling disgust and hurt toward his stepparents for not telling him, as many orphans do when they discover the truth, Lee vowed never to disappoint them or let them down. He never wanted them to regret having adopted him. Lee Majors, having just turned a teenager, went out to prove himself.

He developed his expertise in sports to become a star football player in high school. That led to an athletic scholarship for college. One might suppose that from there he drifted into acting and made it easily with his looks and physique. Not so. While he was playing ball in college, he was suddenly stricken with a latent defect in his spine, resulting in total paralysis from his waist down!

Doctors were divided fifty-fifty over his chances of even walking ever again. So there it was. Seemingly, his football career, his dreams of the future, and his desire to prove himself had gone up in smoke.

Lee Majors wouldn't let them. Two weeks later he stood up. Slowly, painfully, he thought himself into walking again. Finally, he practically forced himself back to near normal. He could run, jump, and even play football, but his time for that had past. He would never again be as good as he was, so it was time for another proving ground, a place to shine.

Lee chose Hollywood. But to too many athletes Hollywood turned out to be a merry-go-round ride to nowhere. A college advisor was reported to have asked him, "Do you really think you have a chance?"

"I've got to make it," Lee replied.

Sure enough, shortly after his arrival Lee had managed to appear on two TV shows as a costar and in two movies. The two films were the late Tom Gries' *Will Penny* in 1968 and *The Liberation of L.B. Jones* in 1970.

Lee with Richard Anderson, OSI's Oscar Goldman.

Will Penny is considered by many to be a near-classic of the Western genre. It starred Charlton Heston in the title role of a cowboy drifter who befriends a widow and her son and then almost loses his life in the process of protecting them from a religious nut and his crazy sons (as played by Donald Pleasance and Bruce Dern, among others).

Lee played Blue, a saddle-bum companion of Will Penny's who arrives to save the day in the nick of time near the end of the film. His role was of the strong-jawed, tight-mouthed variety, so in the reviews there is nary a whisper of him.

In *The Liberation of L.B. Jones* Lee played the pivotal role of Steve Mundine, a lawyer who arrives with his wife in Somerton, Tennessee to try to deal with court cases without prejudice. Needless to say, it doesn't work out, and after various rapes, brutality, and bigotry Mundine leaves town. Again, the critics seemed content to dwell on the film's stylistic shortcomings rather than on any individual performances. Lee fared far better with his television shows.

His first major breakthrough came when he starred with Richard Long and Barbara Stanwyck on *Big Valley,* a Western in the *Bonanza* tradition. Lee portrayed Stanwyck's physical, hot-headed son for about three years until the show petered out from lack of dramatic momentum.

Then Lee secured a position on the staff of *Owen Marshall, Counselor at Law,* starring the fine stage and film actor Arthur Hill. Lee traded the role of Marshall's legman with David Soul after he was signed to play Steve Austin, *The Six Million Dollar Man.*

BACKSTAGE BIONICS

The ninety-minute pilot went down a lot smoother than Col. Austin's test plane at the beginning of the show! Actual footage of a crashing test vehicle was used, by the way, as well as an actual bionic arm borrowed from U.C.L.A.!

The story behind that was that, while the Universal Studios' effects department was whipping up a believable-looking artificial arm to use in the movie, the Medical Center at the California University had actually constructed an incredibly complex limb for their own experimental purposes. So, when Universal got wind of that and it came time to show the interior of the Steve Austin bionic arm, *The Six Million Dollar Man* crew simply borrowed the thing from U.C.L.A. The arm that you saw was a working artificial arm — wire, transistors, and all.

Following that scene Steve Austin leaped to the rescue, crashed through walls, ran at incredible speeds, and lifted huge weights, all in the name of mom and apple pie.

Speaking of running at incredible speeds, Harve Bennett and his crew tested several methods of creating the effect of Steve Austin's superhuman endeavors. They shot at normal filming speed, but the balsa-wood "iron beams" and cardboard "cement walls" look fake when Lee threw or plowed through them. They speeded up the film, but then everything looked funny. Finally, they decided on the present dodge: all bionic accomplishments are filmed in slow motion, accompanied by Oliver Nelson's twanging musical score.

Even though it is a trifle obvious, the style seems to work. I remember a scene when I was teaching a class in Film Special Effects at a Norwalk, Connecticut high school with my good friend, mentor, and fellow author Jeff Rovin (see his *From Jules Verne to Star Trek to Odd John* and *The Supernatural Quiz Book,* also from Drake Publishers).

After forty-five minutes of explaining incredible accomplishments in *2001, The Hindenburg,* and *Jaws,* the only question I got from the students was, "How do they make *The Six Million Dollar Man* go slow?"

For the record. Since films of motion pictures are nothing more than still pictures in succession (twenty-four per second), it follows that, if you take more still pictures in the same time period — say, forty-eight per second — you will see more detail of movement or slower motion. So all they have to do to make Steve Austin run "sixty miles an hour" is to quicken up the camera speed (have it take more pictures, or frames, per second), then show the gauge supposedly recording the speed of the run as sixty miles an hour.

Back to history. The hero-hungry audience reacted to *The Six Million Dollar Man* very well indeed. And where the audience goes, so go the network executives. They ordered more episodes. Bennett stuck to the same basic concept but practically eliminated the adjustment

Again in action, but a little more playful this time. That's his wife,
Farrah Fawcett-Majors, he's carrying with his football.

period. Steve Austin was now fully integrated with his electronic parts, with little threat of malfunction.

Unfortunately, those responsible for scheduling were not so greatly blessed. A.B.C. put Steve Austin opposite *The Mary Tyler Moore Show,* which was like putting Popeye up against Archie Bunker. The youthful audience was not strong enough on that day or time period to bump the outlandish humor and broad audience appeal of the Moore show. The pseudorobot's rating began to drift.

Thankfully, *The Six Million Dollar Man* was soon slipped into the time slot vacated by the failed *Adam's Rib* and the tapped-out *Room 222.* There the bionic power was recharged, and Austin rocketed back to the top twenty.

Lee Majors had finally made it. He was secure, successful, and married to a beautiful and bounteously watchable girl named Farrah Fawcett. Lee had been married once before to a girl whom he met in high school, but that union ended in divorce in 1965 during his struggle to attain acting success. He first saw Farrah in 1968, and they both admit to "love at first sight." But the whole atmosphere was unreal in Los Angeles. Lee was just starting, and visually Farrah appeared to be every man's dream, the golden girl. Lee just couldn't trust his senses, and it wasn't until five years later that they were wed.

And even then everything didn't go smoothly. But more about that later (see the *Charlie's Angels* chapter).

BIONIC BROAD

It wasn't just in Lee's personal life that a woman's touch was considered necessary. For awhile every *Six Million* episode dealt with machismo adventure, giving little room for the Steve Austin character to grow. Lee became a second banana to his stunts.

Harve Bennett was well aware of this fact, having been attracted to the vulnerability and humanness of the concept in the first place. So he had the writers introduce a love interest in a two-part format. A change-of-pace episode that would guarantee a revived interest in Steve Austin and the show.

They came up with one Jaime Sommers, a mysterious, delicate, tawny-haired beauty with whom Steve Austin could fall head over heels in love.

For the role Universal delegated a young actress who was coming to the end of her contract, Lindsay Wagner.

Lindsay Wagner was born June 22, 1949 in Los Angeles, California, city of angels. For her it was a little less. First of all, her parents, Bill Wagner and Marilyn Thrasher, were only eighteen when she was born. Second, they moved around the country with a rapidity that was alarming. As a matter of fact, Lindsay has said, ". . . every time I'd start . . . reading . . . in school, we'd move . . . and I never did learn to read as well as I should."

Thirdly, they had a second daughter, and finally they got divorced when Lindsay was seven. In a way it was just as well. The Wagners were too young, too unhappy, too transient, and Bill had wanted a boy to name after sportscaster Lindsay Nelson. When Lindsay came along, he named her that anyway, which gives you an idea of the consideration that he felt for his own daughter.

Unfortunately, the split didn't make things much better. Neither of the separated parents could afford to support their two girls, so Lindsay was trundled off to her grandmother's house while her mother worked. The house was in a lousy area of town, "a Mexican slum," as Lindsay calls it, and was topped by the fact that the little Lindsay was forcibly given the great responsibility of taking care of her little sister.

"I was trying to grow up myself," said Lindsay," and here I was saddled with helping someone more helpless than I was."

And to all the preceding add the fact that she was five feet, seven inches tall by the time she was ten (yes, ten), and you've got the makings of one whale of an inferiority complex.

"I was the wrong color . . . I talked funny . . . everything was wrong."

Like Robert Blake said, being a kid takes time, and Lindsay just wasn't given any. She was shuffled from relative to relative; she was constantly reprimanded for one thing or another; and she had to take care of other children, a responsibility that even her own mother seemed ill equipped for.

"But," says Lindsay in an article, "because of

Lindsay Wagner as Jaime Sommers, "The Bionic Woman."

that experience I learned a great deal about how to cope with other people.''

That knowledge would come in handy much later, but during her youth it might have been nice to be able to cope with herself and her own problems. Her statuesque height and down-home beauty led her into modeling at the age of thirteen. She also started to take dancing lessons while attending Hollywood High.

Unfortunately, after going through almost every possible dance style Lindsay was graduated summa cum two left feet. And even though Lindsay was working on modeling assignments with the Nina Blanchard agency, she felt the whole thing demeaning. It seems that all the photographers and agents wanted to do was to get her in the sack. Her ethereal beauty and youth seemed to get everyone all excited.

The only other avenue of creative expression left for her seemed to be acting. And at that she excelled. She had a lot of emotion to work off, and, once onstage, she had her chance. She enjoyed the craft; she enjoyed the other people involved; and for the first time it mattered more how good she was than how good she looked.

She began to appear in plays around L.A., where a talent scout for M.G.M. spotted her and offered her a television contract. Fame, fortune, bright lights beckoned. Lindsay turned him down. She knew that she wasn't ready, and her acting instructor, James Best, had convinced her that the better a person she was, the better an actress she'd be.

But all the false starts, stops, and soul-searching had taken a toll on the young girl. By the time her mother remarried and she moved to Portland, Oregon to live with her new parents, Lindsay was nursing a stomach ulcer. She finished her high-school career in Portland, still concentrating on refining her acting skills.

Then came the bum-around period. The sixties saw the birth of the lost generation. Forever questioning the values of their parents and peers, they often had the time and inclination to meander off and investigate a variety of lifestyles. That was exactly what Lindsay proceeded to do. She scooted over to France for two months and bummed around. Then she returned to the University of Oregon and bummed around. Then she practically ran across town, and bummed around the Mount Hood Community College.

As a result of all her bumming around she hooked up as lead singer with a rock group and hit a couple of night spots. The group didn't come to anything, and it was about then that Lindsay drifted back to Hollywood and acting, totally bummed out.

One good thing about her years in limbo was that, beyond the broadening experiences and the education in modern survival, you meet a lot of people who can be of great help once you decide to get constructive. When Lindsay began to reflower as an actress, she called on such acquaintance at Universal who had been encouraging her for a long time and said, ''I'm ready.''

He sent her over to the casting director of *Marcus Welby, M.D.;* she read; and two days later she was taping her first TV show. Sometimes it's just that simple and just that complicated. Shortly after the *Marcus Welby* program was aired, Lindsay was signed to a $162 a-week player's contract. That total shot up somewhat after Lindsay was scheduled to guest on twelve shows in seven days.

By the time she got her first movie role, her salary was about $50,000 a year.

The movie was *Two People* starring Peter Fonda and directed by Robert Wise. In it Lindsay had the thankless role of a cliché-spouting fashion model who has a short affair with a draft dodger. Apparently, Mr. Wise was trying to get back to directing small, meaningful dramas in between the likes of his high-budgeted successes such as *The Sound of Music, The Andromeda Strain,* and *The Hindenburg. Two People* was not the ticket, however, for either Wise or Wagner.

Newsweek said that the movie had ''all the reality of an Air France commercial.'' And ''the husky-voiced Miss Wagner has an oddly beautiful face which is more interesting than the soapy dialogue.''

Time magazine was less kind. They said that Lindsay ''looks as much like a high-fashion model as a drive-in car hop'' and that ''Throughout [the film she] remains a stranger to conviction.'' They were not the reviews that careers are made of.

But that didn't stop Lindsay. Almost immediately after completing *Two People* she was cast as John Houseman's daughter and Timothy Bottoms' love in *The Paper Chase. Chase* traced

Jaime, about to out-maneuver Bigfoot, the legendary California monster.

the career of one student through a year at the Harvard Law school, a place of organized insanity. A place that can drive some to hysteria, some to sickness, and others to suicide. A place where a student can call a teacher a son of a bitch and the teacher will commend the student on his insight.

The film was a moderate critical and financial success, garnering Houseman an Oscar as Best Supporting Actor and Lindsay some mildly affirmative reviews.

But to Universal she was one pretty girl among many. One executive is reported to have said that she was "just another tall, skinny broad with no boobs." So the studio decided to let her contract run out and release her. But then, seemingly just to squeeze as much as they could out of her last days, they cast her as the love interest in a two-part episode of *The Six Million Dollar Man*.

BIONIC REBIRTH

Lindsay Wagner called her mother. She said, "Mom, they've offered me the silliest script." When her mother found out the name of the program that the script was for, she said, "But that's your sister's favorite show." On the strength of that argument Lindsay reconsidered, "O.K. I'll read it again."

She read it again, and it's amazing to think that without Lindsay's sister this chapter wouldn't be as long as it is.

The two-part segment, for which Lindsay was paid $25,000, was filmed. Bionic boy meets bionic girl. Bionic boy saves girl. Bionic boy loves girl. Bionic boy loses girl in sky-diving accident. Bionic boy's boss tries to make bionic girl. Bionic boy loses bionic girl when bionic body rejects girl. The music swells; Steve Austin leans over the dead Jaime on the operating table and tenderly kisses his love on the forehead. The end. There isn't an unrusty bionic part in the house.

The final shot was in the can five days after Lindsay Wagner's contract had expired. Lindsay and Universal parted company. Good, said Steve Austin, I can get back to the good stuff now that this mushy stuff is all over. Good, said Jaime Sommers, my alter ego always wanted to be a movie actress anyway.

But then the mail came in. And then the ratings

came in—thousands upon thousands of letters admonishing the network for killing Jaime and demanding her back poured in. There was even a letter from a doctor saying that A.B.C. had to do something about the kids that it had traumatized in his hospital. The rating for that particular segment went through the roof or to the moon or into orbit, depending upon whom you talk to and how far-out their imaginations are. The response was clear. A.B.C. had to resurrect Jaime Sommers and fast.

A.B.C. called Universal. Bring back Jaime. Universal called casting. Get us that Wagner girl. Casting called back. What Wagner girl? You mean the one we just released . . . uh-oh . . . .

I can just imagine the sinking feeling in Universal's collective stomach. Supposedly, Universal bandied other actresses' names about to play Jaime, including Sally Field and Stephanie Powers. One source even claimed that Lee Majors suggested his wife Farrah. But A.B.C. was definite in its choice: Lindsay Wagner.

So Universal began to court Lindsay's affections to get her back. But Lindsay was ready with a chaperone. Ron Samuels, an agent-manager whose clients have included Evel Knievel and Charo, took on Lindsay's case and the Universal execs. It was an extraordinary situation that combined monetary chutzpah with desperation.

Lindsay figured that she had nothing to lose, so she and Samuels asked for five hundred thousand dollars a year, a 12½% interest in all *Bionic Woman* products, and a guarantee of at least one major-motion-picture role a year for every year that her show is on. Universal, figuring that they had everything to lose, gave it to her.

Supposedly, no one was more surprised than Lindsay. And she didn't even want to do TV! But it didn't stop there. A sudden case of bionic envy popped up. The story goes that Lee Majors, supposedly angered and hurt by Lindsay's walking up and taking the golden fleece after he had struggled for years just to get near it, announced a veritable boycott against the new show, refusing to guest on it. But Lindsay had no argument with Lee. Given time to cool off, Lee realized that, if he were going to get mad, he might as well save up his anger for the next time that he and A.B.C. had contract talks.

Beyond Lee's supermacho chagrin one actor was very happy with Lindsay's success. Richard Anderson, the man who plays Oscar Goldman,

No, Jaime doesn't have bionic eyes, but then again, she doesn't seem to need them. Here, she stares knives at an acquaintance.

the OSI director and control for both bionic folk, was working too much to feel bad. Richard is the first in this TV-spinoff world to be a permanent double agent. That is, he plays the same character in two shows at once.

And not because he needs the money, either. He's a veteran of the golden days at M.G.M. as well as an actor of great versatility up to the very day of his casting as Oscar.

Many of you might remember him in *Forbidden Planet*. More recently he has appeared in the ridiculous and the sublime. The ridiculous being *Kitten With a Whip*, *The Ride to Hangman's Tree*, and *Macho Callahan*. The more sublime being *Seven Days In May*, *Seconds*, and *Tora, Tora, Tora*.

Even if all Richard Anderson's film roles were ridiculous, he wouldn't have to worry. Not only does he have the money from these parts but the rewards of two oilwells that he invested in to live off. Richard is sitting pretty and happy.

And what does he think of his two companion stars? Well, Lee and Richard go quail hunting together. Lindsay and Richard have dinner together and respect each other immensely. It is a pleasure for all of them to be working in solid hits.

The Six Million Dollar Man remains strong with or without love interest. Bennett has wisely chosen to loosen up the Bionic Man themes, so one week Austin can go on a deadly mission, and the next week he can get involved with raising a tough street kid.

And *The Bionic Woman* is a hit! And Lindsay Wagner is almost an overnight superstar. How does she cope with such sudden overwhelming acceptance? Lee has a strong and beautiful wife to keep his equilibrium, not to mention his own determination. What does Lindsay have? Two things, actually. One is the Arica Institute, and the other is a man named Michael Brandon.

The Institute is in New York, and its purpose is to help people handle problems by making them take an inward look at themselves rather than blaming their difficulties on others. Michael is an actor and screenwriter whom Lindsay met at an acting workshop even before she became the Bionic Woman.

And, like Lee and Farrah, it was mutually admitted love at first sight. The story goes that Michael simply walked through the door when

Lindsay was in the room and their eyes locked. They just stared at each other. Lindsay couldn't take her eyes off him. Michael, who had thought that he would never find true love, knew that this was it. They sat down together, each feeling a special electric attraction.

Michael is one of those character actors who can go from one role to the next with an almost invisible versatility. He doesn't worry about leading role or supporting: he does them all and does them well. You may have seen him in any number of movies, such as *Lovers and Other Strangers*, such as *Queen of the Stardust Ballroom*, and *The Red Badge of Courage*.

The day after he and Lindsay met, he had to go on-location in Hawaii, but, when he returned, he called her, picked her up, and brought her out to his ranch, and they stayed there for a month. It, indeed, was love.

It is very hard to be in love in a town like L.A. The word itself is bandied about everywhere and used to describe everything. The life is so fast and false that knowing when the real thing comes along is difficult and keeping it sometimes seems impossible. But the two, Brandon and Wagner, have experience, understanding, and conviction. And they are both individuals able to interact humanly together. They know that what they have is special and unique.

At first they were both deliriously happy. They had so much to share as people, and, finally, each had someone special to share it with. Then the accident happened. Afterwards Lindsay couldn't understand how she had caused it. The car was too wrecked to check for mechanical error, but Michael is sure that it was caused by Lindsay's intrinsic exhaustion.

The Bionic Woman had been on the air for awhile. Lindsay was driving home with Michael in their small sportscar on a warm, sunny afternoon. The road wasn't wet and a tire didn't blow out, but suddenly the car was on its right side, off the road and smashed into a tree.

Lindsay remembers waking up with people over her and hearing a man say, "Her face, what about her face?" She figured that that was it for her career. She turned and saw in the rearview mirror that she had three lips. She turned away and saw Michael unconscious with his face bleeding. She finally looked up at the tree until she lost consciousness.

Lindsay doesn't have to look worried. She's already gotten Universal Studios to cough up more than a half million a year.

Jaime in the ring, but not about to take the fall!

The two were rushed to the U.C.L.A. Medical Center, the same place where *The Six Million Dollar Man* crew found their original bionic arm. There a Dr. Sillsby, a remarkable plastic surgeon, conferred with Ron Samuels on their condition Ron made it clear that, without their faces, their careers would be over. Dr. Sillsby, with that information in mind and his special kind of genius, went to work.

He handled all of Lindsay's head wounds without creating a single scar. He rebuilt Michael's eyebrow on the operating table, since Brandon had smashed into one of the sportscar's convertable roof clips. Michael was left with a hardly noticeable "arrow" on his brow as a souvenir, while Lindsay had only to look at her love to be reminded that she had almost killed her reason for living. Both were lucky to be alive; both knew it; and it brought them even closer together.

Even though Lindsay wanted to be free of commitments before they married, and both wanted nothing in the way of their life together, not TV, movies, or anything, the two were wed at the beginning of this year. They had learned that love doesn't and can't and shouldn't wait. When it is important enough to share your life for — well, it's important enough to share your life for.

BIONICS BUPKIS

The woman from the broken home is on the verge of starting her own life with a man she loves and a firm conviction based on mutual respect and love.

Meanwhile, Lee Majors has a new feature film in the works and has done a movie for N.B.C., telecast last year, entitled *The Francis Gary Powers Story*.

Bionic fever continues to sweep the country. Three series of Bionic books fill the racks. The first by Martin Caidin, the original author; an adaptation of *Six Million Dollar Man* scripts; and the third, a female-authored *Bionic Woman* series. Steve Austin and Jaime Sommers dolls are cleaning up. And a *Bionic Boy* series may go on the air at A.B.C.!

Thanks to Lee and Lindsay, two superheroes of the seventies are staying strong.

Jaclyn Smith, Farrah Fawcett-Majors, and Kate Jackson as "Charlie's Angels."

CHARLIE'S ANGELS AND WONDER WOMAN

(or wonder angels and charlie's women)

Jaclyn Smith as Kelly
Kate Jackson as Sabrina
Farrah Fawcett-Majors as Jill
Lynda Carter as Wonder Woman

A strange thing is happening in the world of TV fandom. For years parents were forced to change from their news programs. basketball games, documentaries, and dramas on the public-broadcast stations so that their daughters could watch the "dreamy" Illya on *The Man from U.N.C.L.E.* or the gorgeous Bobby Sherman or even the cool Edd Byrnes on *77 Sunset Strip*.

Basically, teenage idols were the exclusive area of females. Men had nothing to do but marvel at the depth of their girls' passion for the various superstars, wonder what they had that they didn't, and hope that the girls would grow out of it soon.

But today, as I said, a strange thing is happening. In this age of gender and genre awareness, in this age of women's consciousness, in this age of the equal-rights amendment, the women's lib movement is paying off for male-chauvinist pigs in spades. Not only do the girls come down to interrupt parental viewing and rave over The Fonz, Barbarino, and *The Six Million Dollar Man,* but the *guys* come down on Wednesdays and Saturdays and rave over certain other attractions. And more often than not the daddies stay too. Suddenly, however, the wives and daughters find something to do in the kitchen.

In the past women on TV didn't have much to recommend them. When they weren't nurses or secretaries, they were bopped around or bumped off on various crime shows. Occasionally, a "woman's show" would come along, but most often these shows pictured either silly house-wives or mindless mannequins. No, the male population couldn't see much in the likes of *Gidget, Bewitched,* or Carol Burnett. About the only place where the imaginative American male could turn to for fantasy realization was a British show, *The Avengers,* with Diana Rigg as Emma Peel.

The delightful Mrs. Peel (her husband was lost up the Amazon before the series started), usually encased in some sort of clingy leather bodysuit, would bash around sundry international baddies or be threatened with various vicious extinctions until the suave John Steed (played by Patrick MacNee) would appear in bowler hat and um-brella to save the day.

Even then we guys had merely her long, dark locks and feline temperament to stoke the fuel of our passion. To be blunt, her body was no great shakes. As a matter of fact, she was downright thin. We wanted somebody substantial. A heroic figure that we could get our eyes into.

MMMMMMM

WONDER WOMAN

Lynda Carter

Born:

Place of Birth: Phoenix, Arizona

Educated: Arcadia High School

Titles: *Miss Arizona-World*
Miss World-U.S.A.

Height: 6' 0"

Weight: 130 pounds

Hair: Black

Eyes: Gray-green-and-blue

Hobbies: Singing

1970's network television provided not one but four. Beyond the worth even of Mary Tyler Moore, Rhoda, and Phyllis. Above the abilities of Laverne and Shirley and the Bionic Woman. Better than the contributions of Pinky Tuscadaro, Rosie, and Aunt Bluebell are Kelly Garrett, Sabrina Duncan, Jill, and Diana. Commonly known as *Charlie's Angels* and *Wonder Woman*

Wow! One isn't sure whether their bounteous presence, all on one network, all during one season, is a huge step forward for women's lib or a huge step back. For, on the most part they are hardly fulfilling a woman's dream. Even though their plot lines revolve around succeeding in a man's world, they are presented almost solely for the pleasure and approval of the male viewer.

And they don't have to worry about getting it, either. Suddenly, rabid fan worship has become a family affair. Little brothers can counter little sister's posters of the Sweathogs and Starsky and Hutch with Farrah Fawcett-Majors and Lynda Carter. Adults can unabashedly view comic-book plot lines and teenage entertainment. Who are these gorgeous girls and how did they congregate on TV all at once?

Well, as usual, we have A.B.C. to thank. The entire network has shucked any sort of pretension and unreservingly given the American public what it wants. They have hit so many targets with a bullseye all at once that it seems unreal. First *Happy Days, Kotter,* and *Starsky and Hutch;* then *Rich Man, Poor Man* and *Roots.* Something for everyone, a little bit of this, a little bit of that. Truly an incredible showing.

CHARLIE'S ANGELS

Charlie's Angels come from the fertile mind of Aaron Spelling, the fastest pen in the West. The man plays his hunches with the skill of the best riverboat gambler. A book on fan favorites wouldn't be complete without him. He might be the biggest, best, and most influential fan of all.

Fan, according to Webster's dictionary, in its third usage means an enthusiastic devotee or, an ardent admirer or enthusiast. And Aaron is nothing if not that. He's an enthusiastic devotee of writing and an ardent admirer of success. His finger has been on the pulse of the nation for quite some time, and he can read symptoms as well as the best doctor.

ANGELS

Farrah Fawcett-Majors

Born: February 2, 1957

Place of Birth: Texas

Educated: University of Texas

Hair: Blonde

Eyes: The color of fallen leaves

Height: 5' 6½"

Weight: 112 pounds

Hobbies: Sculpture, painting, tennis

———

Jaclyn Smith

Born: October 26, 1950

Place of Birth: Houston, Texas

Educated: Trinity University

Hcight: 5' 7"

Weight: 111 pounds

Hair: Brown

Eyes: Brown

Hobbies: Dance, water skiing, horses,
    teaching

Kate Jackson

Born: October 29, 1948

Place of Birth: Birmingham, Alabama

Educated: Birmingham Southern University

Film: *Thunder and Lightning* (with David
    Carradine)

TV: *The Rookies* (with George Sanford
    Brown)

Height: 5' 8"

Weight: 124 pounds

Hair: Brown

Eyes: Blue

Hobbies: Traveling, reading

Address of all four: c/o ABC
    4151 Prospect Ave.
    Hollywood, Cal. 90029

His earlier television prescriptions have included *The Mod Squad, The Rookies,* and *S.W.A.T.,* as well as countless TV movies. So where did he come from to be so smart?

He was born on the bad side of Dallas, Texas to a poor tailor who worked night and day to support him and his brothers and sisters. Aaron read like crazy as a boy and began to write like crazy in high school. From there he wrote like crazy at Southern Methodist University, where he was the first playwright since Eugene O'Neill to win two Harvard Awards for the best original one-act play.

Afterwards, almost by natural extension, he moved to directing while continuing to write like crazy. Besides completing thirty-six plays in three years he directed full-time at three different Texas-area theaters, each year winning the Critic's Award for Best Southwest Director.

So what happened? What turned the driven cerebral creator into A.B.C.'s main proponent of schlock entertainment? New York, that's what. There they didn't care how good or talented you were; the New York theatrical world world ate talent. They trounced on idealism. They buried good intentions under tons of ego, red tape, poverty, and garbage. Though he was still writing like crazy, it took a job with an orchestra to get him to L.A. and into show business.

He was hired by Ada Leonard to take the group's instruments on- and offstage. But Aaron didn't mind. It was money, and it took him across the country.

Once secure on the West Coast, he won the Hollywood One Act Play Contest and kept himself going by becoming an actor. He worked in television shows and movies while waiting, strangely enough, for his big writing break. It came though the intervention of Alan Ladd.

Ladd was one of those tough but sensitive actors who have been all but forgotten as the years passed. Names such as John Garfield and Alan Ladd were lost in the glow of names such as Bogart and Cagney. But then Ladd was one of the best. His pictures, such as *This Gun for Hire* and *The Glass Key,* will long be remembered by lovers of the mystery genre.

Ladd hired Spelling almost immediately after reading one of his scripts. And from there Aaron's ferocious output was nearly matched by demands from the studios. He wrote hundreds

upon hundreds of scripts. For the *Zane Grey Theater, Playhouse 90,* and many others. He kept working, growing, and writing like crazy into the sixties, when he met Elton Rule, the president of A.B.C.

Over a lunch meeting Rule simply said, "Trust me." Aaron did, and here he is today. Cleverly, soundly forming hit after hit. Whether or not you like his choice of subject matter or his almost mercenary way of capitalizing on an idea, you can't argue with his success. Whatever your own personal conviction may be, there are countless millions out there who agree with Aaron Spelling.

And that's good, because *Charlie's Angels* might very well be the most mercenary of all. Here is a show, purportedly in answer to all those he-man, macho, all-male cop shows (such as *S.W.A.T.* and *The Rookies),* bought, sold, and packaged for the single purpose of creating drool. By getting three gorgeous, sexy girls for the leads, then creating plot lines that have them in and out of as many revealing costumes as possible the makers of this show have ensured an all-male, macho, he-man audience response.

Farrah Fawcett-Majors, one of Charlie's angels, jokingly put it this way when she was asked about the skyrocketing ratings: "I thought it was purely because of our acting ability. Now that we're number one, I think it's because we don't wear bras." So the girls knew what they were getting into. Let's get to know the girls.

Jaclyn Smith

Jaclyn Smith is Kelly, the gal with the shady past and the come-on grin. She is the one who is usually called upon to do the most bathing-suit displaying, thanks to a solid body attuned by studying ballet since she was three.

She was born in Houston, Texas, and her father was a dentist, so she must have lived in a better section of town than Aaron Spelling. She grew up well and strong, thanks to dance lessons, and, after finishing at Trinity University in San Antonio, California, she headed to New York, where she became a model and taught dance with the Head Start program for underprivileged kids.

Soon she decided that the best work was available in L.A., so she moved to Beverly Hills, bought a house, and set up shop. It wasn't long before *Charlie's Angels* beckoned. Meanwhile,

Jaclyn Smith as Jill.

she is still thinking about teaching children again, and her dog, Albert, is reportedly well known and loved on the set.

Jaclyn seems to be the least understood member of the trio. Her character is the only mysterious one and often becomes fuzzy when compared to the unique and attention-getting personal lives of the other two. But according to all reports she's happy, quiet, well off, and unattached. Watch your local channel for further reports.

Kate Jackson

Kate Jackson is Sabrina, the earth mother, the supposed intellectual, even though she is called on to do only the most rudimentary thinking on the show. However, she is called upon to do most of the hitting and hazardous driving and to get dangerously bopped. Because she's the least fragile-looking of the three. Her body is slim, not sensual (well, at least not to the degree of the others). Her grin is sharp, not come-hither. Her eyes twinkle, not smolder. And her attitude is more aggressive, thereby both exciting and threatening at the same time.

Kate's drive had garnered her more attention than her career. She is almost universally pictured in articles and interviews as a sharp cookie. And that's one of her main problems, it seems. She's too good-looking to be appreciated as a person. She's either a morally vapid operator or a cute chick with delusions of grandeur. Sources just can't seem to agree.

Kate is always being portrayed through the shortcomings and hangups of her portrayers.

On the personal side, she was born in Birmingham, Alabama, went to high school and Birmingham Southern University there, and must have worked a whale of a lot on eliminating an accent or "pecularities of speech" in order to make it in show business.

She traveled a lot—to Italy, the Caribbean, and England — before she settled in Los Angeles to fight for success. And she fought for success in the company of several notable dates. The Hollywood gossips seem to love fueling the flames of her reputation by snapping pictures and suggesting rumors of Kate with Bob Evans, the maverick producer and ex-love of Ali MacGraw, or Kate with Edward Albert, the rising star and son of actor Eddie Albert.

But it seems that Kate will have none of it. Her career reality won't live with the pursuit of dates. Edward Albert was in *Midway, Butterflies are Free* (with Paul Michael Glaser) and the upcoming *Domino Principle,* but you don't see her in the cast list of these pictures, do you? Robert Evans made *Chinatown, Marathon Man,* and *Black Sunday,* but she's not in those, either.

No, Kate's first film is under the auspices of Roger Corman, the self-same man whom Ron Howard is working with. Corman has been torturing the major studios for years by making millions of dollars on cheap adventure and soft-core erotica, while the studios wheeze under monstrous, expensive flops.

To add to the insult, Corman also heads New World Pictures, the company responsible for bringing the great cinematic works of Frenchman François Truffaut, Italian Federico Fellini, and Swede Ingmar Bergman to this country. Without Corman *Day for Night, Amarcord, Scenes from a Marriage,* and *Face to Face* might never have been seen or raved over on American screens.

So now major studios have begun hiring out Corman as maverick producer on action-exploitation pictures. Twentieth Century-Fox has two of Corman's bullet-riddled, car-crash-filled, action-packed movies on their 1977 schedule: *Moving Violation* and *Thunder and Lightning,* the latter starring David Carradine (TV's *Kung Fu* and movie's *Woody Guthrie)* and Kate Jackson. The two play southern moonshiners who run afoul of everything but the kitchen sink.

Unlike the other two, Kate has more than modeling experience to fall back upon. She played Jill Danko, one of the wives of *The Rookies,* for four years under the production hand of, surprise, Aaron Spelling. On that show she played a nurse, and, when she wasn't simply responding to various doctors and policemen, she was invariably threatened with rape, terror, or extinction by sundry psychopaths. Unfortunately, on that show she was mostly forced to scream and bear it, so it must have been a pleasure to haul off and sock the sucker, like she gets to do on *Charlie's Angels.*

Farrah Fawcett-Majors

And now we come to Farrah Fawcett-Majors. The girl whose picture adorns at least four million

Kate Jackson as Sabrina.

walls. The girl with at least three hundred fifty teeth gleaming brightly out of a smile that would make Count Dracula feel anemic. The girl seemingly is almost too good-to-be true. What must it be like for a shy girl to suffer through such mindless adulation? How is someone to deal with the sad fact that, for a majority of her young life, she is to be considered a thing instead of a person and that, for the rest of her mature life, she will be thought of in terms of what she was instead of who she is?

Basically, it comes down to three things. Either accept it and become what others think you are, fight against it, or ignore it and try to be yourself. Seemingly, Farrah has been able to do a little of all three.

She was born in 1947, the daughter of a Texas oil millionaire. Because of her upbringing she was part of a group that accepted her beauty and sometimes downright expected her to be beautiful. But if part of her upbringing was pretentious, the rest was cultured and intelligent. Farrah grew up shy but civilized. She began to broaden her creative horizons in high school, where she sang in the concert choir and learned sculpture.

It was in her freshman year at the University of Texas at Austin that she was voted one of the Ten Most Beautiful Girls on Campus. Her picture was sent to Hollywood as a result, and she was invited to come out to try her luck by a publicist. On this trial run she met Lee Majors and began a relationship and a career both of which would culminate in five years.

Farrah soon became easily recognizable simply on the strength of her commercials. Her incredibly unique eyes shone on either side of a strong, straight nose; large, gleaming teeth shone out of a full mouth; and a huge head of blonde hair with a life of its own encircled the entire visage.

Men everywhere wanted to run out and buy hair conditioner when her face appeared under a waterfall; Joe Namath had his face lathered with shaving cream by her; her teeth gave an honest meaning to toothpaste with sex appeal; and presently she's rising out of oceans and dropping out of helicopters to strip her outerwear so that we all see her TR7. It's enough to eliminate commercial-break icebox raiding.

In 1973 Farrah married Lee Majors after a half-decade bout of "love-at-first-sight-too-good-to-be-true" blues. They were very happy together, each fulfilling needs and fantasies in the other.

They were married and in love. A plus B equals C. But then all the Ds and Es and Fs started to get involved. No one in Hollywood seems to want people to be happy. Happiness makes for contentment, not for news, so the rumors started circulating. Lee was falling in love with Lindsay Wagner. Farrah was too busy to be a good wife. The two were having all sorts of trouble, from Lee's fragile ego to Farrah's exhaustion.

To squelch the foolishness, Lee took out a page in *Variety,* declaring that he and Farrah were very much in love and had never been happier. That was good for a few laughs to the Hollywood press. More rumors about how insecure and childish the act was were circulated. You can't seem to win in Hollywood. The cloying headlines continued: "Lee and Farrah, Playing with Fire," "Can Charlie's Angel Compete with the Bionic Woman?" (the answer to those questions are "no" and "yes," by the way).

But the Lee-Farrah love affair continues as well. After their first date Lee sent her thirteen yellow roses. His consideration and gallantry continues. He bought twin Mercedes with phones so that they can talk to each other on location. Farrah made sure that being released by seven in the evening was part of her contract so that she could spend evenings with Lee. She also made her stage name Farrah Fawcett-Majors so that everyone would know where her loyalties lay.

Meanwhile, her royalties pile up in the bank. The big question now is how the relationship will fare under Farrah's new-found popularity. Will two stars in the house be too many? Again, look to the skies, as they said in an old horror movie, for the answer.

I wouldn't worry that much about the longevity of *Charlie's Angels,* however. Even though the three girls are most probably here to stay, a show based on little more than quickly glimpsed flesh will probably not last that long. After awhile, without quality of style or writing, the great majority of viewers will look to something different, something that rewards them more than just visually.

The same flesh in the same story week after week, year after year, is bound to get tiring. And

Farrah Fawcett-Majors as Kelly.

therein lies the pity. It is too bad that they didn't take the idea and make it into a program that says something or at least has a style of presentation with more meat to it. As it is, *Charlie's Angels* is worse than a Chinese meal. Five minutes after it's over, you're hungry again.

The plots don't stand out; the acting doesn't stand out; the gimmicks are worn. It is a shame that such a original idea was showcased on a show that isn't good, isn't bad, but just gorgeous.

WONDER WOMAN

Lynda Carter, Heavens to Betsy, Lynda Carter. Six feet of pure, pulsating womanhood. It's hard to believe that the small TV tube can hold her. A true bounty of all good things. So enough snide male-chauvinist ravings, already. Many would agree, I'm sure, that, physcially, at least, she is a true wonder woman.

Well, back to the comic books, eh? Charles Moulton didn't like the way comic books were treating females during World War II. Even while America's female population was in the factories, riveting, welding, keeping the country strong, sacrificing so that the boys fighting overseas would win, the female population in the comics was still getting captured, still making stupid mistakes, and still being saved by the likes of Superman, Batman, and Captain America.

So Moulton figured that it was about time to give the little girls all over the country someone to root for. So Wonder Woman premiered in *All Star Comics,* in December 1941. By 1942 she had her own book, a daily comic strip, and a huge following. Not only had Moulton tapped the secret fantasy of countless girls, but he created the first great media women's libber. A superpowered Germaine Greer.

And he was well equipped for it, because Moulton turned out to be a pen name for none other than William Moulton Marston, a famous psychologist and developer of the lie detector! Marston not only got a percentage of the action but scripted the *Wonder Woman* series as his soapbox on modern male-female relationships.

The original story was this. Mars, the god of war, and Aphrodite, the goddess of beauty, were at odds with one another over who would rule earth. Mars wanted men with swords to be tops. Aphrodite wanted to conquer with wo-

men's love (isn't that just like a woman?). But Mars wouldn't be swayed. His swordsmen created the ancient world of cruelty and slavery.

Aphrodite responded by creating a race of superwomen, whom she named Amazons, and a magic belt that would make the wearer unconquerable! But after several sound defeats Mars hired Hercules to get the belt away. Herc tried to beat it out of the Amazons but got severely trounced for his troubles. So then he used the old standby, false love. He romanced the leader of the Amazons, thereby stealing her heart *and* the belt. Mars took his opportunity and overcame the now mortal ladies. The women were soundly defeated, captured, and enslaved by Mars' minions.

Aphrodite called down from the heavens: "You may break your chains. But you must wear these wrist bands always to teach you the folly of submitting to men's domination!"

So the Amazons escaped and went to Paradise Island, a place no man knew of. There, under the guidance of another goddess, Athena, *Wonder Woman* was fashioned as a baby statue that came to life. You heard it here first.

Anyway, the *Wonder Woman* strip succeeded beyond anyone's wildest dreams. National Periodicals, also known as D.C. Comics, handled the series to this very day, along with *Superman, Batman, The Green Lantern, Flash,* and many others. But DC fell upon hard times in the sixties when Stan Lee's Marvel Comics line hit the stands. The old-fashioned stories and heroes weren't making it with the in crowd. More three-dimensional, neurotic heroes were the going thing. So when Warner Communications bought out National, it was a welcome occurrence.

Then Universal's *Six Million Dollar Man* came along. Warner's thought, boy, if they can have a comic-book hero, so can we! So they produced a *Wonder Woman Movie of the Week* with some basic but important changes.

First, they modernized the story line so that they could have Steve Austin-like adventures. Second, they thinned, softened, and covered the girl playing *Wonder Woman* up.

They hired Cathy Lee Crosby, a slim, delicately bored blonde, to play the part, wearing a drab one-piece jumpsuit. It might have worked for *The Bionic Woman* later, but it didn't work

The girls get together for one more shot.

Lynda Carter as the mighty "Wonder Woman."

Kathy Lee Crosby who played the first "Wonder Woman," throws a spear.

for *Wonder Woman* now. And last, the script and the direction were awful. Worse, they were boring. I couldn't accuse even the pilot of *Batman* of being that.

The original 1974 pilot of *Wonder Woman* wasn't sexy—it wasn't anything! Cathy Lee did hardly anything worth a magic belt, and the villains were about as thought-out as the swine-flu-vaccination program. A great disappointment at best, yeech! at worst.

Warners still thought they had something here. They told Douglas Cramer and Bud Baumes to find out what. Upon investigation Cramer and Baumes were taken with the charms of the original comic. First, it took place in the age of innocence when you could tell the good guys from the bad; second, it had women's-lib overtones; third, the heroine offered a chance to put real sex appeal on television.

Cramer was reported to have described whatever girl they cast as "built like a javelin thrower but with the sweet face of . . . Mary Tyler Moore." Then a vice president of Warner's said: "Sure. We'll cross-pollinate Olga Korbut with Godzilla."

Meanwhile, as they say in the comics, Lynda Carter was all grown up and just waiting to be discovered. She had been born twenty-five years earlier in Phoenix, Arizona, the daughter of an antiques dealer. And she had grown up fast, too. By the time she went to Arcadia High School she was taller than almost everybody except the teachers and the football players. And very well endowed as well.

Lynda sought to fit in with her talent. She took singing lessons and wrote music until, at the age of fifteen, she was asked to join a singing group called Just Us.

Following that were other gigs and other groups, which lasted three years after her high-school education ended. But soon the club dates stopped, her associates drifted off, and the last note rattled away. Lynda returned to Phoenix.

Bored, she entered a 1972 beauty contest. Well, there aren't many like her back home, no matter where you live. Sources say that the reaction was strong and immediate. She won. And went on to the Miss Arizona—World and the Miss World—U.S.A. pageants. After a year of reign, Lynda moved to L.A. and began acting lessons. There her path crossed with Douglas

Cramer's. But not for very long. Almost immediately they were walking in the same direction. The second *Wonder Woman* movie was under way.

The plot took up where my synopsis left off. Diana, the immortal Amazon (no mention of her birth by statue was made) was growing up happily on Paradise Island until Major Steve Trevor, U.S. Air Force, crashed on their beach in 1942.

In the original comic Diana saves his life by zapping him with a forbidden purple healing ray. In the movie, however, he is just nursed back to health. Not as exciting, maybe, but less confused.

It seems that a war is going on and the ruler of Paradise Island decrees that an Amazon must go and help the side of right win. She announces a tournament to decide which one should go. Diana wins, and she is presented with a star-spangled bathing suit, the magic belt, bracelets that can deflect bullets, and a lasso that, when used, forces the roped person to tell the truth (shades of Moulton and his lie detector!).

The now wonderized Diana takes Major Trevor back to the States in her invisible plane and takes up the battle against evil and Nazis (in 1942 they were one and the same). Naturally, she needs a secret identity to protect her, so she becomes Yeoman First Class Diana Prince, secretary to Steve Trevor (and how she got past all the necessary experience and paperwork to become a Yeoman in the Armed Forces I'll never know).

Supposedly plain-looking with her hair up and wearing glasses, Diana hangs around the office giving sound advice until an emergency comes up. Then, getting off alone, she spins around, there's a huge flash of light, and voila! *Wonder Woman* in all her glory! And I do mean glory.

The show was successful when it was aired in November 1975. Besides the obvious attraction of Lynda the show was good. The script by Stanley Ralph Ross was tight and humorous, the extra touches by Cramer were intelligent and enjoyable, and the direction was fast and well done. The action was well handled and considerable, and there was a fight scene near the end that was simply marvelous.

That should have done it. *Wonder Woman* should have been optioned as a show by A.B.C. and introduced into their schedule. Instead it

Lynda doesn't bother with spears. She prefers modern weapons.

Back by popular demand, "Wonder Woman" is now a top-ranking show.

took the advances of the two other networks to show A.B.C. that it cared. C.B.S. was interested in the possibility of a competitor with *The Bionic Woman* and tried to buy the series. A.B.C. didn't bite, extended its option, and commissioned two more *Wonder Woman* segments. In July it was suddenly announced that N.B.C. would option the show from Warner's and put it on the air on the coming new season. But only if A.B.C. didn't renew its option.

A.B.C. knew that it had a good thing. About a week or two later A.B.C. made clear its intention of scheduling and airing *Wonder Woman* specials in different lengths on different days and at different times. It must have been a ball for Lynda to have three networks fight over her.

Basically, though, *Wonder Woman* is now seen on Saturdays at eight and is unfortunately changed. The format is the same, but the style for the most part is gone. The action has become more and more stilted and occurs less often; the plots have become near uniform, barring a gimmick or two; and the humor is practically non-existent.

But it still has Lynda Carter. And all she needs is a little help from the writers and directors, and *Wonder Woman* will be with us for a long time to come.

The cast, from the left: Phil Foster, Michael McKean, Penny Marshall, David Lander, Cindy Williams, and Eddie Mekka.

LAVERNE AND SHIRLEY

(beer-blanket bimbos, or two schleps at shotz)

Cindy Williams as Shirley
Penny Marshall as Laverne
Phil Foster as Laverne's Father, Mr. DeFazio
Eddie Mekka as Carmine
David Lander as Squiggy
Michael McKean as Lenny

Amidst the morass that is network television, among the variety of programming fare, cop shows, doctor shows, soap operas, game shows, comedies, and dramas, betwixt the quality of viewing, good, bad, and indifferent, is a show so different in style, so unusual in presentation, so odd in format, so strident and crazy that sitting and watching it is like tuning into another world (and I don't mean the soap opera).

Characters come and go like a rapid-fire sub-machine gun, jokes tumble out like a raging flood. Situations form, take shape, and carry on hilariously before your disbelieving eyes. Sophisticated slapstick is not dead. Two rising princesses have it well in hand.

The plot line of this show is deceptively simple. Two girls, who work in a beer brewery in Milwaukee during the fifties, try to find love and happiness. *That* is a plot line for a successful show? Who on earth would enjoy a comedy like that? Well, maybe the same people who liked a show about a redhead married to a Cuban bandleader in New York. Or a variety show starring another plain, skinny redhead whose main character is a mute washwoman.

None of these concepts seems very promising on paper, but, when you introduce certain names and personalities, everything comes together. The variety show, Carol Burnett. The redhead married to the bandleader, Lucille Ball. And the two brewery girls? Laverne DeFazio and Shirley Feeney. DeFazio and Feeney? Even the names are unusual. Of course, we all know them better as Penny Marshall and Cindy Williams, the two gifted actresses and comedians who star every week in the *Happy Days* spin-off *Laverne and Shirley*.

So what makes their show different? What catapults the program light years ahead of its spin-off qualification? For the answer a little background is required. *Happy Days* had exploded into its third season. The Fonz was the reigning king of television, and the stories on the show were following suit. Episodes featured Fonzie's past, present, and future and were charted out for his millions of fans. Pretty soon his personal relatives and friends were introduced. His great aunt, his little nephew Butch, the Polanski twins, and two of his old girlfriends, Laverne and Shirley.

The *Happy Days* writers had created an episode in which the depressed Richie Cunningham asked for help and guidance for his lack of womanizing ability from The Fonz. It seems that

LAVERNE AND SHIRLEY

Penny Marshall

Born: August 15, 1944

Place of Birth: Bronx, New York

Parents: Tony and Marjorie Marshall

Educated: University of New Mexico

Films: *How Sweet It Is!* (with Erin Moran)
    The Savage Seven (with Adam Roarke)

Height: 5' 6"

Weight: 123 pounds

Hair: Sandy brown   Eyes: Brown

Hobbies: Needlepoint, jigsaw puzzles

Address: c/o ABC
           4151 Prospect Ave.
           Hollywood, Cal. 90029

Cindy Williams

Born: August 22,

Place of Birth: Van Nuys, California

Films: *Gas-s-s-s* (with Ben Vereen)
    Travels with my Aunt (with Vanessa
      Redgrave)
    American Graffiti (with Richard
      Dreyfuss)
    The Conversation (with Gene
      Hackman)
    The First Nudie Musical

Height: 5' 4"

Weight: 105 pounds

Hair: Brown

Eyes: Blue

Hobbies: Cards

Richie was striking out constantly and had lost faith in himself. So The Fonz comes up with the idea of going out on a double date with two chicks whom he knew. Later at Arnold's Drive-In, with Richie waiting anxiously, in walk two of the toughest, brassiest, loudest girls Richie had ever seen.

One was a petite brunette who strove at all times to be sophisticated but kept letting her uncouth nature slip out. The other was a sandy-haired semivulnerable banshee whose fists spoke louder than words. As a matter of fact, halfway through the following scene the girls get into an

argument about the proper way to act and go to the ladies' room to slug it out.

Such was the first introduction of *Laverne and Shirley*. Where on earth was Gary Marshall and his crew going to find the right combination of uncouth comedy actresses to play such unsubtle roles?

Well, for Laverne Gary didn't have very far to look. His own sister, Penny, had just the right amount of ability and brassiness to play the part. All he had to do then was to get through her inferiority complex enough to agree to play the role. Marshall also knew another young actress

*The girls together in their Milwaukee bedroom.
Shirley jogs while Laverne disapproves.*

with enough spunk and character yet different enough from Penny to play Shirley. But again, he had a tough time convincing her, because she was a movie actress and didn't want anything to do with television.

But finally, on the basis that it would be only a one-spot deal, a temporary thing at the very most, both girls agreed to do the episode. It was magic. They came off as more than guest stars, they stole the show! Letters began to pour in, asking who were these girls? Where did they come from? When will we see them again?

Well, it's about time in this here narrative for some answers.

PENNY MARSHALL

Penny Marshall, the daughter of Tony Marshall, a television producer, and Marjorie, his wife, was born on October 15, 1944. She had a big brother, Gary, who wanted to follow in his father's footsteps, and they all lived in the Bronx, New York. Right across the street from them lived the Reiner family, father Carl and little Robert, but, as is often the case in neighborhoods, the two families didn't really get to know each other until much later.

As little Penny grew up, the shy, introverted one of the family, she started to follow in her mother's footsteps by learning to dance. Her mother had been a dance instructor for years, so, like almost everything else in the Marshall's life, her ability was "all in the family."

Every summer Penny went to a Jewish day camp, and every year she went to a nice school with a lot of Jewish people, so all Penny seemed to know was what her peers taught her. Grow up, learn to cook and sew, marry a nice Jewish boy, and settle down. Even though she believed in it, Penny didn't excel at any of it.

When it came time to go to secondary school, Penny enrolled in the University of New Mexico, majoring in math, psychology, and recreation. She had thoughts of becoming a dance teacher like her mother. Below the border all of a sudden there were men who weren't short, curly-haired with big noses. There were tall, blond men with big, blue eyes.

Penny went wild. She stuck by some rules that she still held sacred in her subconscious, but she went bonzo. The culmination of this was that she

got married in Albuquerque, New Mexico when she was nineteen.

"All those rules we were taught," Penny remembered: "Don't beat the guy at anything, let him win, remain a virgin, get married . . . I didn't question it. I accepted it."

It wasn't long before her tenuous union split up. Penny had always been insecure, and the divorce led her to believe that she was no good.

She began to forcefully demean herself. Her reality only seemed to strengthen her poor image of herself. She was young and divorced, not a good sign to many people. Mothers wouldn't let their sons date her. Guys thought she was only after one thing. I mean, *you* know about divorced women, right?

So Penny left college, began to teach dancing, and participated in a light-opera company. "To meet men," she insists. Finally at the end of her rope, she called her brother Gary out in Hollywood and asked if she could stay with him. Gary was climbing the ladder of TV success, but a sister was a sister, so he made a place for her in his home and in his career. Gary saw that there was great sensitivity and style beneath Penny's dunky-seeming exterior, so he got her a part on *Love, American Style* and, by alternately praising and cajoling her, got her on the soundstage. Afterwards, Penny professed that she thought she looked "gross" on the episode.

To keep busy while Gary worked, Penny also appeared in two movies in 1968. The first, for her brother, was called *How Sweet It Is,* and costarred a young girl named Erin Moran; the second was a motorcycle blood-and-guts epic for Dick Clark called *The Savage Seven*. It was bad, but it wasn't boring.

A little later Gary and Jerry Belson were deep into the third season of *The Odd Couple* with Tony Randall as Felix and Jack Klugman as Oscar and needed a change of pace. So they built the character of Myrna, Oscar's secretary, around Penny and got her back on TV sets.

It was about then that she met Rob Reiner in a West Hollywood club. Rob had been making his way as an actor and writer, whipping up material and appearing in his father's movie *Where's Poppa?* He took immediately to this "swan in ugly duckling's feathers." After a crazy courtship the two were married in a singular wedding ceremony in which part of Penny's self-written

The mighty mouth of Lenny with Squiggy tuning out.
David Lander (left) and Michael McKean.

vow was, "I'll always be your best friend, and I'll try not to make you nervous."

A special *Odd Couple* episode was written around Rob and Penny's relationship in which Myrna's swinging-bachelor boyfriend decides he loves Myrna for who she is, not who he might think she should be. The two obviously have a strong and giving marriage.

After *The Odd Couple* was cancelled and *All in the Family*, with Rob as Mike, was entrenched in the top ten, Penny got involved with the M.T.M. production company, guest-starring in their stable of shows. Such as *The Mary Tyler Moore Show, Bob Newhart,* and *Friends and Lovers*. Not so commonly known (to me, anyway) is the fact that she auditioned for Gloria on *All in the Family* but was the only girl reading who looked like Edith. All the others were blond and buxom. The producers picked Sally Struthers. At that stage in her career came the call to play Laverne DeFazio.

CINDY WILLIAMS

Cindy Williams was born cute. She was born cute on August 22 in Van Nuys, California. She was born cute to parents with a conservative farming background who couldn't think of anything worse than to have their daughter consider going into acting. But that's what she wanted, all right.

She knew that theater was the career that she wanted to follow even when she was very young. She and her parents had "discussions" about it from Austin, Texas and back, but finally Cindy's "yeses" were stronger than her parents "nos," so she won out. And ever since that day has been speaking her mind unreservedly and definitely.

In high school she had no trouble with her career or her personal life. Her charm and energy had matured, so she had no trouble getting dates, while her talent developed, so she had no trouble getting roles. She also spent some time writing and directing. Her only mistake of those years, she felt, was to go with boys who were attractive and that's it. Usually, they had no character, charm, or anything. But Cindy's own warmth made up for it.

After college Cindy took on Hollywood with a one-track mind. She was going to be successful, and she was going to do it her way. No selling

out, she convinced herself. She began slowly by appearing in little theater productions by night and working as a waitress by day. Then she started feeling out the industry with guest roles on *Room 222, Hawaii Five-O,* and others.

She slowly moved toward films, getting involved with a whole group of talented young people under the production control of Roger Corman. What? Again? Yup, Roger Corman. One of Cindy's first movie roles was in the Roger Corman-produced and -directed *Gas-s-s-s, or It May Become Necessary to Destroy the World to Save It*. This was a charming story about a governmentally created nerve gas that killed off everyone in the world over twenty-five. The gist of the film was that some young idealists prevented a fascist football team on motorcycles called Jason and the Nomads from destroying El Paso. The climax included thunder and lightning, Che Guevara, earthquakes, Edgar Allen Poe and his raven, and Jesus. It may not sound like much, but you had to be there.

Even though it was a very unlikely groundbreaker, this movie not only showcased the talents of Cindy but those of Ben Vereen and Talia Shire as well. It also enabled Cindy to meet the likes of George Lucas and Francis Ford Coppola, two very handy people in her upcoming career.

Cindy continued working, securing the role of Tooley in *Travels with My Aunt,* starring Vanessa Redgrave, before she was called on to portray Laurie in *American Graffiti,* written and directed by George Lucas. Even then Cindy was being careful. She thought that she looked and was too old to play a sixteen-year-old high-school junior. Francis Ford Coppola urged her to try it, so she tested with her costar, an eighteen-year-old actor named Ron Howard (small world, isn't it?).

Naturally, Cindy got the part, and, as we all know by now, *American Graffiti* was a smash. Following that it took very little convincing for Cindy to do Francis Ford Coppola's *The Conversation* with Gene Hackman, Robert Duvall, Allan Garfield, and John Cazale. First of all, it was a gigantic change of pace, and secondly, it was a powerhouse film. *Time* described it as having "enormous enterprise and tension"; the actors were "meticulously casted."

In short, it was the story of a professional bug-

Penny Marshall as Laverne DeFazio.

ger, a surveillance man, who was suffering from a severe case of moral paralysis. He has eavesdropped and taped a conversation between a girl and her lover in a park and then begins to believe that someone is trying to kill the duo. He discovers by the end of this draining, electrifying film that things are never as they seem.

Around the time that Cindy was working on *The First Nudie Musical*, a soft-core pornography satire, she got the call to do Shirley Feeney.

SUCCESS

The *Happy Days* production team had decided. If Norman Lear and Mary Tyler Moore could do it, so could they. It was spinoff time. The writing crew began producing scripts; the word went out to suitable directors, and Gary Marshall contacted Cindy and Penny.

Cindy was on the unemployment line. No! she replied. Penny was at home with Rob, panicking. I don't want to, was her attitude. The *Happy Days* creators worked on Cindy. They'd make the character of Shirley more interesting. They'd introduce interesting themes. The show would have substance. Aw, c'mon, please, just this once?

Rob sat Penny down and had a long talk. He knew that she could do it. She had doubts about her ability and attractiveness. Rob knew that she would be great. Finally, it came down to the bottom line.

As Penny put it, "I'd rather go through the grind of a weekly series than sit at home filled with insecurity and boredom."

Cindy succumbed as well. As long as the show was decent, it would be money and would probably lead to more parts. I mean, who's going to want to watch two caustic, dumpy-dressed girls who work in a brewery anyway? Both girls started work thinking of the series as a midseason lark, a show that wouldn't last more than thirteen weeks. On that basis *Laverne and Shirley* was born as a weekly series.

The show was a successful hit smash! The gritty, hilarious misadventures of the two wildly different career girls at the Shotz brewery caught on. It was so warm, human, and funny that it rolled across the country like a beer keg. The public took the tough, wisecracking Laverne with her monogrammed shirts and the idealistic, romantic Shirley to their collective breasts.

With that basic foundation the creators built an entire world around their two "diamonds in the rough." Laverne's father is played by veteran comedian Phil Foster; their apartment house's landlady is played by Betty Garrett, late of *All in the Family*; and, for conflict's sake, Laverne is matched against the big mouth and big bank account of Big Rosie Greenbaum, unflatteringly played by Carole White.

Laverne and Shirley's coworkers at the plant and upstairs neighbors are Lenny and Squiggy, two of the oddest characters on TV since Bullwinkle and Rocky. The two, Lenny and Squiggy (not Bullwinkle and Rocky), are portrayed beautifully (if you can call card-carrying craziness beautiful) by Michael McKean and David Lander, two pals since college days.

David, the short, dark-haired one, was born in Brooklyn, raised in the Bronx, and educated at the United States' premier theatrical institution, Carnegie-Mellon in Pittsburgh. It was there that he met McKean, the tall, blond one. The two participated in some heavy acting experiences in Pennsylvania, still keeping their nutsy demeanor, until David split for Hollywood. There he held a variety of jobs until his versatile voice was pigeonholed for three years on a radio station. That was when Michael trotted over to the West Coast to join his friend, and they put together a radio comedy spot. They hung around and made friends with Penny and Cindy, so, when the possibility of funny neighbors came up at a production meeting, the girls immediately recommended Lander and McKean.

Michael explains that the characterizations of Lenny and Squiggy are based on guys whom we all knew in high school, the little, greasy nerds who always thought they were so great. Both he and David do a magnificent job of keeping their roles fresh and likable, and it might not be surprising if TV viewers saw a lot more of them.

And finally, there's Carmine Regusa, the Big Ragu, as played by Eddie Mekka. Carmine was originally introduced as a love interest for Shirley but was soon changed into a friendly advisor to both the girls as well as one of the finest street gigolos in Milwaukee. If you need anything, from

In 1973, Cindy Williams adored Ron Howard in "American Graffiti."

hot jewelry to an abortion, the Big Ragu knows where to get it. He's an opportunist with a heart of gold, though.

Eddie comes well equipped to play the clever, singing Italian even though he's really Armenian. He spent his youth singing, opera mostly, until he won a scholarship to the Boston Conservatory of Music. From there Eddie hit Broadway, looking to combine his love of music with his interest in theater. His six years of dance lessons didn't hurt, either. He got a Tony Award nomination for his work in *The Lieutenant* and then toured the country with Hal Linden, who won a Tony Award for his starring role in *The Rothchilds*.

Eddie's search for meaty roles brought him to Hollywood, where he did a few commercials. Almost immediately, he signed with an agent, and the producers of *Laverne and Shirley* called. It happened just that fast: Eddie was on and creeping into your hearts.

Laverne and Shirley was in the top ten shows, the girls were displaying a love for each other, and the material we all shared. It wasn't until the producers noticed that *Laverne and Shirley* were jumping around a lot that they got a real fix on which direction the series was going in.

Simply doing funny lines and going from one place to another didn't seem to be enough for the girls. They didn't seem to be truly alive unless they were doing some sort of physical slapstick. The show started to bring out howls of delight only when something wild and unpredictable happened.

So "expect the unexpected" became the watchword on the new *Laverne and Shirley* programs. Now it isn't unusual to see Laverne swinging back and forth on a refrigerator door or Shirley leaping across the room of a ritzy hotel to pounce on a Ritz cracker. Or even for the girls to go into a wild bossa nova, rumba, or tango number as "dime-a-dance" girls.

It also isn't unusual for a girl to pull a switchblade, for a fox stole to be dunked in punch, or for Rosie Greenbaum to be smacked in the face by a bowl of spaghetti and meatballs. The show has become brilliantly bizarre and in some cases almost downright perverted.

How long they can keep the masterly inventive material flowing is anyone's guess, but as long as they do and as long as Penny Marshall and Cindy Williams keep acting, *Laverne and Shirley* will be up there among the best of them!

Now it's just beer bottles. Cindy Williams as Shirley Feeney.

Donny and Marie Osmond catch you in the web of their happiness.

THE DONNY AND MARIE SHOW

(or the six-million-dollar molars)

Donny and Marie Osmond
The Osmond Family

There is a very weird show on Friday night. While the rest of television seems to be made up of raucous comedies, violence, innuendo, greed, and horror, this one show is packed with undiluted joy, love, music, and good times. There are no double entendres, no wicked sexual comments, no lascivious natures. Instead there are costumes, sets, spectacle, music, and an ice ballet per week.

Backstage no smoking, drinking, swearing, or even coffee is allowed. And all around are the smiling, peaceful members of one family, taking care and making sure of almost everything. What is it, a Hare Krishna telethon? A King Family retrospective? Charlie Manson discovering est (that's in bad taste)? No, it's the Donny and Marie Osmond show. The place where, if the wholesomeness doesn't get you, the pure candlepower of the smiling will.

Yep, Donny and Marie Osmond, the seventh and eighth of a family of nine, all under the guidance and steady religious hands of George and Olive Osmond of Utah.

It all began about 1960 when Merrill, Wayne, Alan, Jay, and Donny first appeared on the *Andy Williams Show* as the Osmond Brothers. Virl and Tom, the other two Osmonds, were born, unfor-

tunately, with serious hearing impairments and were unable to sing—at least, on key—with the boys. From that day on Donny was denied a normal young life, trading it in instead for something much more exciting. Superstardom.

The Osmonds were greatly appreciated by Andy Williams' viewers, so they stayed with the show off and on and between their successful personal appearances through the sixties. For awhile they were the vanguard of good, clean-singing groups: The Cowsills, The Partridge Family, and others followed in their wake. But then the seventies exploded into view, with acid rock and soul music. A new family was exploding onto the scene. The Jackson Five, a black group with their own brand of drive, was wiping out the Osmonds' staid and mellow approach.

But the Osmonds weren't down for long. Donny had grown up into the most personable of them all, and the only girl, Marie, was discovered to have a clear, strong singing voice. So the group traded in their thin ties and small-lapeled suits for white-spangled jumpsuits and amplification.

The new Osmonds burst into view with Donny firmly in the lead. The WASP population found itself enjoying them without worry or guilt. The Osmonds were back on top again.

131

DONNY AND MARIE

Donny

Birthdate: December 18, 1955

Height: 5' 10"

Weight: 130 pounds

Age: Nineteen

Marie

Birthdate: October 10, 1957

Height: 5' 5"

Weight: 100 pounds

Age: Seventeen

Home: Provo, Utah

Parents: George and Olive Osmond

Brothers: Virl, Tom, Merrill, Wayne, Alan, Jay, Jimmy

Pets: Dogs, cats, horses

Hobbies: Skiing, skating, karate, cooking, electronics, reading

Address them: c/o ABC
4151 Prospect Ave.
Hollywood, Cal. 90029

Around 1973 Marie was introduced, a plaintive thirteen-year-old, singing *Paper Roses*. From then on she and Donny were thought of as a team. They symbolized the young, squeaky-clean kids whom parents wish they had and whom kids wish they could be.

Naturally, as their newfound fame grew, network interest grew as well. After successful appearances on several other shows the production team of Sid and Marty Krofft, basically known for their Saturday morning show *H.R. Puffinstuff*, signed Donny and Marie for their own prime-time variety show.

But when you sign one Osmond, you sign all the Osmonds. And the whole family couldn't be more welcome, for Sid and Marty specialized and believed in family entertainment.

Sid has said: "They're the most incredible people . . . that I have ever known . . . Their minds just flow together on one beautiful path. They can do anything."

And indeed they do. Not only did Donny and Marie learn to ice skate for the show, but they can dance, tap, play almost any instrument between them; Jay Osmond choreographs, the two nonsinging brothers handle the fan club; the rest of the Osmond brothers orchestrate; and the parents handle most of the business end.

As Sid Krofft further elucidates, "When you talk to one, you talk to all of them."

But doesn't all this togetherness lead to friction and resentment? Can a person be given so much so fast without psychological damage? With the fast life and pressure, can the Osmonds really be happy?

It seems so. For the secret is in the upbringing and in the past. Every one of the Osmonds is a member and believer in the Mormon Church and ethic. In this religion honesty is held above all else. To yourself, to others, and to God. This sets up certain rules, which mean no junk food, no cursing, no dating until the age of eighteen, and no sex before marriage. The belief, intelligence, and goodness of the family continually prove their way of life a successful one. By all outward appearances the family loves each other very much. George has created the Osmond Foundation to help both blind and deaf children as well as donating ten percent of the entire family income to the Mormon Church.

Even with the restrictions on the set guest stars

Evel Knieval joins them on ice.

Donny and Marie, season one, Marie with long hair.

continually come away from the Osmond-show soundstage with nothing but respect and admiration for the entire clan. The most jaded and cynical often can't deny, after a period spent among them, that their devotion and love are indeed on the level and deeply felt.

So who are the two stars of the Osmond family? What are their likes and dislikes? What makes them tick? Well, performing makes Donny tick. He's been doing it since he was four, and he professes to love it. He doesn't think in terms of what he's missed: he thinks in terms of what experience he's gained and what fun he's had. Because even though he's been on the go almost his entire life, his education and interest haven't been ignored or skirted.

He's had the best education the family could afford, and Donny's become something of an electrical wizard. He's done extensive wiring at their Virl Osmond-designed home in Provo, Utah, including automatic-control TV buttons, electric-eye light switches, electronic door closers, and many others. Basically, Donny's the kind of guy who once something interests him, learns all he can until he feels he knows it. Recently his extracurricular pursuits have included karate and skiing.

Marie likes to think of herself as just another normal girl. Who just happens to sing, has eight brothers, and is part of a multimillion-dollar family empire. But her family and its wealth only allow her to maintain her femininity. Where else could she simply pursue her quest to be whoever she wants with such devotion? People who know her describe her as sensitive, caring, polite, and feminine to the point of cooking, cleaning, and sewing around the Osmond house.

So the Osmond family is incredibly talented, incredibly happy, and incredibly rich. When they are not doing *The Donny and Marie Show*, they are tending the Osmond fan club, scheduling and completing whirlwind Las Vegas and national show tours, participating in Mormon Church activities and functions, and pursuing their goal of bringing happiness to the world.

CHICO AND THE MAN

(in memory of/rest in peace)

It's an old, old story by now. How we all sit at home, watching the TV stars, wishing we could be like them. And how they wish fervently that their lives were a little more normal, how they wish they were like us.

But we never believe them. We can't. It's *they* who have it all. It's they who have a bounty of everything we want. We would trade places with them in a second, right?

Then something happens. A person's life is shattered, a man's wealth is gone, a woman's career turns up hollow and empty. It's splashed across our faces in words and pictures for all to see, but we still cannot believe it. It still isn't real for us. I mean, these people exist only for our entertainment, right? They are merely servants of our fantasies, right? Then they go home to their big houses, swimming pools, love, and money, right?

How can any of *them* be unhappy? It is not possible. We simply cannot believe it.

Man, what a wreck. It's like we're all standing around his grave, waiting to get interviews. I sit in my office, surrounded by the final remnants, the articles, the books, the obituaries of a man named Freddie Prinze.

He's been dead for at least five months now, but once he actually lived in our world for twenty-two years. Hell, that makes me older than him.

Actually, it really wasn't our world that he lived in. Although I was an actor for twelve years, a cartoonist for two, a writer of five books, and a stand-up comedian in Boston, it wasn't like it was for him. I mean, at the age of twenty he was at the top.

He had gone from the Manhattan High School of the Performing Arts right into a major contract at the age of eighteen, to successful nightclub routines, then onto *The Tonight Show*.

Suddenly, he was headlining in Las Vegas, and he was signed by James Komack to be the star of an N.B.C. network comedy. He had the fame that he had dreamed about, wealth he never imagined, and trouble beyond measure.

Freddie Prinze wasn't ready for it. I know, you might be asking yourself, how can anybody *not* be ready for that? Well, like a friend of mine once said, "When you're at the bottom, you had better be happy, because that's all you've got." But when you're at the top, you have a variety of choices. And the only way is down.

Robert Blake, *Baretta*, talked about what it's

137

like. What it is like to step from the dirty streets into the unreal world of success. For Blake it took the form of a dream that he has. The dream can take place anywhere, at any time, but "wherever you are, you don't belong. That everybody else has got it, but you ain't got it. Everybody else has the equipment. But they can see what you are. They can see because you're . . . naked. They can see."

You don't belong. You don't have it. And everybody knows it. It makes no difference how much talent you have. It makes no difference whether it's true or false. As long as one thinks it's true, it's real. From all reports Freddie Prinze thought it was true.

He said it when he was a kid in school. He always had high marks; he learned to read and write faster and better than almost everyone in his class; but he still felt that he didn't belong.

He said it in Hollywood. He said it wasn't his style, that it made him feel as if he had no right to be there. He even said it in Washington after he performed at the pre-Inauguration gala for President Carter. Less than a week before his death.

Freddie Prinze was remembered by his few friends in New York as a "chubby little white kid" who used to get beat up a lot. And he was universally recognized as crazy. He would constantly crack up his neighbors with jokes and impersonations. He was also the best putdown artist on the block.

Even so, he didn't really fit in. He wasn't athletic, he wasn't good with girls, and he wasn't very happy. So he drifted deeper into a dream world of his own making. He would tell whopping lies and make up fabulous stories. He would fantasize about being everything from a disc jockey to a spy.

Freddie Prinze made his break into the real world of fantasy by enrolling in the High School of Performing Arts. There he learned how to perform. How to be someone other than himself. And he participated in the deadly fantasy world of pushing drugs.

He categorized himself as crazy during those years. He dealt in marijuana, blasted himself up with cocaine, then smashed himself down with Valium. Finally, he couldn't take it anymore and tried to commit suicide by overdosing. He only got very sick.

Freddie Prinze seemed to come out of his fog

on his feet after that, but those who knew him best saw that he was never free again. Besides continuing to pop sedatives Prinze's personal life was a mess. He was part child and part man. And by continuing his comedy appearances, nightclub acts, and guest spots he didn't have to deal with it. He escaped through fantasy.

Freddie Prinze got married in September 1975 to a girl named Kathy in Las Vegas. Reportedly, they hardly knew one another when they were wed. They had a child together, but their union lasted only fourteen months. Prinze's life was sinking deeper and deeper.

We all know how this story ends. I'll get to it. It was about four years since he had started his career. He was back in L.A. after visiting the White House and our new President. It was January 26, 1977. After all the investigations, after all the articles, after all the eulogies, the last days of Freddie Prinze's life went like this.

He was picked up at James Komack's house by a girlfriend named Suzanne to go over to see his psychiatrist, William Kroger. During the ride over Prinze pulled out a gun, a .32 caliber revolver. He joked about it, then put it away. At Kroger's house Suzanne begged the doctor to take the gun. He did and put it in his safe. Prinze stayed at Kroger's house that night, and the next day he had the gun again.

He rehearsed a new episode of *Chico and the Man*, then drove over to meet his personal secretary, Carol Novak, at his apartment in the Beverly Comstock at about 6:30 P.M. He had popped five Quaaludes and washed them down with wine by the time he arrived.

Within minutes Prinze was asleep on his couch. Novak made and answered some phone calls. She called Dr. Kroger. She answered when Kathy called. Kroger called back. It was 9:00 P.M. on January 27. Prinze awoke and talked to Kroger. He checked his supply of pills and the gun. He played backgammon with Novak. He called Kathy, because the next day was her birthday. Then he said, "I'm gonna do it," a couple of times. He hung up the phone, had two more Quaaludes with some wine, and tried to play some more backgammon. He asked Carol to hug him because he was lonely.

Shortly after that he was up and giving instructions. He was making a mental list of things to do

Freddie Prinze, 1954 - 1977.

*On "Chico and the Man" with his co-stars
Jack Albertson and Scatman Crothers.*

the next day, since they were going to tape that week's *Chico* episode. Then he took two more pills and put the .32 in his pants pocket. Prinze's personal manager called at about 1:00 A.M. Dr. Kroger arrived later that morning. They talked about Freddie's personality and his future well-being. Carol Novak decided that it was safe to go home.

Then Kroger left. Prinze still had the gun. He called Dusty Snyder, his business manager, who rushed right over after calling Novak. Prinze called his mother and told her that he was going to do it. His mother called Novak in a panic. Novak called Prinze. Prinze answered and told her that Snyder was with him and that he was going to do it. Then, cryptically, he began going over his mental schedule with her again. Prinze hung up.

On the morning of Friday, January 28, 1977, his ex-wife's birthday, Freddie Prinze took the .32 revolver out of his pocket, put it up to his head, and pulled the trigger.

And we still can't believe it. We weren't there like Dusty Snyder. We weren't at the funeral. The only Freddie Prinze we knew was the one we saw on television. The only evidence of his death we have are words on paper. Our only tie with his demise is the fact that he won't be on *Chico* anymore. Unless there are reruns. He won't guest-host *The Tonight Show* anymore. He'll never be on another Las Vegas marquee.

But others will take his place. Like one drop in the ocean, we'll hardly know he's gone. Abundant talent will still star in Vegas. Doc Severinson, Ed McMahon, McLean Stevenson, Flip Wilson, Joey Bishop, Bill Cosby, Don Rickles, Steve Martin, and others will still guest-host *The Tonight Show*. Comedians will still come and go. We'll all still laugh.

But Freddie Prinze was once a living human being. And, damn it, he was only twenty-two years old. His friends and relatives can't understand how he could take his own life. One said that he had it all and threw it away. But that isn't true. He had it in his hands and he didn't want it. But instead of chucking it and walking away something in him made him hold on until it got so heavy that it crushed him.

I can't say whether he'll be remembered. I can't say whether his story is important. I can't say whether it means something. All I can say is that Prinze was a casualty and that he doesn't care anymore. For him it's over.

*Nick Nolte, as viewers of "Rich Man, Poor Man," like him,
in trouble and in action.*

WORLDS FOR THE ASKING

Rich Man, Poor Man
Captains and the Kings
Honorary Mentions
Other Stars To Look Out For
The Game Shows
Cult Worship

The cheers have died down, the ovation trickles away, the music fades, and the curtain falls. Then, one by one, the supporting players make their appearances, accompanied by a polite smattering of applause, slightly louder when an outgoing audience member spots one of his favorites.

1977 has been an incredible year for superstars. More have appeared in this one year than in almost the last five. And they are lasting, having for the most part talents that far exceed the limitations of their various roles.

Henry Winkler will star in *Heroes* with Talia Shire. John Travolta will be in Robert Stigwood's *(Tommy) Saturday Night,* directed by John Avildsen *(Rocky),* as well as recreating his Broadway roll in *Grease.* Gabe Kaplan did an episode of *Police Story.* Cindy Williams and Penny Marshall have a record album of 1950s songs out.

And there are others. Other men and women who have made an incredible impact and are just bubbling under the surface of superstardom, waiting to explode over the top. You have seen them, and you'll see more as the year goes on.

PETER STRAUSS

The only surviving character of the *Rich Man, Poor Man* fictional trio, Peter played the pivotal role of wealthy Rudy Jordache with gusto. Gusto fed by his own talent and a five-hundred-thousand-dollar-plus-a-year contract!

"I've got a better deal than Lindsay Wagner," he was reported to have exclaimed.

Until recently just another of those countless good-looking actors whom nobody hears about, Peter was born in New York's Hudson River Valley to a German wine importer. He got hooked on acting in high school, developed his habit at Northwestern College, and finally rushed off to Hollywood immediately after his graduation in 1969. Where he went through an actor's cold turkey of a sort.

"I can't say that I've gone broke . . . but there have been days when I didn't work," Peter was heard to admit.

So he partook of the on-again, off-again world of the young, rising actor, making a little money here and there in any creative way he could.

He worked in films, such as *Soldier Blue* with Candice Bergen, a bloody tale of Indian persecution in the old West, and *Hail Hero* with Michael Douglas, a dreary story of teenage alienation. He worked on TV in *The Streets of San Francisco, Cannon,* and *Medical Center.* Anything to keep him, his wife Beverly, their dog Beowulf, and their five hundred cactus specimens from going under.

"I've certainly paid my dues . . ." Peter says, "but I've loved everything I've done."

He first heard about *Rich Man, Poor Man* five years ago when Beverly was reading the Irwin Shaw novel and told him that there was a perfect part for him in it. Half a decade later he was in the studio, reading for the part of Rudy while Nick Nolte auditioned for Tom. They both got the job, and *RM, PM* was a ground-breaking success. In its wake have come *Roots* and the N.B.C. series *Best Sellers*.

"When I . . . landed the part of Rudy, I was thrilled and surprised," Peter admits. "But my wife wasn't surprised in the least. She had that certain feeling all along."

Follwing that smash Peter found himself in an excellent bargaining position for the upcoming season's TV sequel. As he had previously noted, Lindsay Wagner had set the precedent for price; the A.B.C. execs were desperate for him, since his costars, Nick Nolte and Susan Blakely, had turned the continuing series down; so Peter simply followed his best intuition.

So far Peter has been working on the scripts with the writing staff and reaping in the monetary benefits of his stardom. He is confident that he will leave the series in the good hands of his costars, James Carroll Jordan and Greg Henry, at the end of the season and go on to other things. But at the same time he's worried. Everybody has been telling him that he has to be extra careful about his next role. They all consider the second break to be the key to continuing success. Even so Peter is controlling his doubts.

"The role of Rudy Jordache is my job . . . My role at home as a husband . . . is my life. Nothing is going to interfere with that. That I can promise."

NICK NOLTE

Thousands of *Rich Man, Poor Man* viewers went into catatonic shock last year when Tom Jordache was gunned down in the closing minutes of the twelve-hour marathan TV production. Tom had grown as a character and as a person to many viewers and was accepted and loved. To have him killed off before their very eyes was like watching the death of a friend.

Letters and phone calls assailed the A.B.C. studios. The studio executives were rubbing their hands and gloating. The ending had its de-

sired effect. Now all they had to do was sign up the young actor playing Tom for the next season. They would figure out how to bring him back from the dead later.

But the young actor wasn't buying. Nick Nolte said no! After a month of pounding America's psyche Nick wasn't about to undercut his popularity by being resurrected. He had been waiting too long for artistic freedom to let it blow away by doing the "safe" thing and staying on television. No, he took his money and ran.

Memories of all the potboilers he'd been in, such as *Return to Macon County,* on his way to the top were fresh in his brain. Safe and secure at his ranch in Agoura, California, Nick took steps to ensure his future career.

First, he signed for *The Deep,* a twelve-million-dollar movie directed by the action expert, Peter Yates *(Bullit, The Hot Rock, Friends of Eddie Coyle). The Deep* is the second novel by Peter Benchley, the author of *Jaws.* It concerns a young newlywed couple who get involved with sunken treasure, drug smuggling, voodoo, and violence on a Caribbean island. Also in the cast are Robert Shaw, Jacqueline Bisset, Eli Wallach, and Lou Gossett. It will be released in nine hundred theaters on June 11.

Second, Nick set up a production company with his long-time business manager. On their agenda is a three-part miniseries called *Who's Eddie?*. Nick will star as a man reexamining his life in a small midwestern town.

Tom Jordache was a gambler in *Rich Man, Poor Man.* Nick Nolte in reality is not much different from his character. He's shooting his whole wad on a movie career and betting on success. No one who knows him thinks that he'll end up like Tom Jordache.

The rest of the networks didn't take their time. With *Rich Man, Poor Man* an unexpected success, it wasn't long before N.B.C. had a show like it in the works. They figured that, if the audience liked one "novel for television," they'd *love* a whole series of them. So they didn't fool around. They secured the rights to four hefty books and began production.

RICHARD JORDAN

Spanking new and ready for the autumn of 1976 was *Captains and the Kings.* Taylor Caldwell's

Richard Jordan from "The Captains and the Kings".

sweeping depiction of an Irish Catholic immigrant's rise to power, wealth, and influence was the first to be scheduled. So the word went out: "Get Beau Bridges for the lead." When he couldn't do it, N.B.C. considered a variety of actors, but then, three days before filming started, they settled on a "semiknown" quantity. Richard Jordan.

Jordan was a known classical actor who was making a reputation by appearing in unsuccessful movies. He did a more than creditable job in all of them, playing diversified parts, but since the movies didn't take off, casting directors somehow blamed him partially.

Richard was an opportunistic federal agent in *The Friends of Eddie Coyle* with Robert Mitchum, a teeth-grinding psychotic rustler in *The Cowboys* with John Wayne, and a close-minded cop of the future in *Logan's Run* with Michael York.

But it took television and *Captains and the Kings* to give him a breakthrough. For the show he had to age almost fifty years, with the help of the makeup department, and his acting left audiences and coworkers alike amazed. Now critics are calling him the new Richard Burton.

Douglas Heyes, the screenwriter and director of *Captains,* calls Richard, "The only actor I ever worked with whose scope is unlimited."

Jordan grew up with everything and knew what he wanted always. The grandson of a famous judge, Richard went to the best schools, from Hotchkiss to Harvard, but practically always knew that he was going to be an actor with or without the education. He went through all the expensive schooling only because he felt that he "owed it" to his parents.

From Cambridge, Massachusetts Richard returned to his home stomping grounds of New York and studied with Harold Clurman and Sandy Meisner, two well-known acting teachers, until he went under the wing of Joseph Papp, the revolutionary New York play producer. Richard appeared in seven years of Shakespeare for Papp.

His first role was that of Romeo. On and off stage his Juliet was an actress named Kathleen Widdoes. Soon after their thespian meeting they were married in Paris. But soon after that they were divorced. An actor's life is not easy, secure, or unemotional.

As Richard says: ". . . my material is emotions. Emotions are what I paint with."

And, with two actors in the family, a breakup seemed inevitable. Especially since Richard has been described as somewhat of a chauvinist. Women's lib came along and washed their union asunder.

"Marriage," Richard was reported to have said, "is out now. Almost nobody I know is married."

But that isn't to say that Jordan isn't happy: "I'd like all the love I can get," he says, "all the money, all the parts, all the happiness. I'd like to live forever . . ."

In acting, however, just as in all the other creative arts, there always seems to be an edge on success. Richard recognizes this.

"I'm having a good time now . . . I don't want to get zapped."

HONORARY MENTIONS

(1) Al Molinaro of *Happy Days* (Al)
(2) Pat Morita of *Happy Days* (Arnold)
(3) Bernie Hamilton of *Starsky and Hutch* (Dobey)
(4) Ed Grover of *Baretta* (Brubaker)
(5) Tom Ewell of *Baretta* (Billy)
(6) David Doyle of *Charlie's Angels* (Bosley)
(7) Lyle Waggoner of *Wonder Woman* (Steve Trevor)
(8) Jimmy Walker of *Good Times* (J.J.)
(9) Richard Thomas of *The Waltons* (John-Boy)
(10) *The Captain and Tennille*
Darryl Dragon
Toni Tennille
(11) *Barney Miller*

Hal Linden	Jack Soo
Ron Glass	Steve Landesberg
Max Gail	James Gregory
Abe Vigoda	Linda Lavin

(12) *The Brady Bunch*

Robert Reed	Florence Henderson
Mike Lookinland	Eve Plum
Barry Williams	Maureen McCormack
Christopher Knight	Susan Olson

(13) *The Jacksons*
(14) John Amos of *Roots*
(15) Mary Tyler Moore

Peter Marshall, host of "Hollywood Squares".

OTHER STARS TO LOOK OUT FOR

(1) Sam Elliott of *Once an Eagle* as Sgt. Damon
Tall, dark, and handsome, this southern actor has paid his dues with movies such as *Frogs* and hopes for the big break that he didn't get in *Lifeguard.*

(2) Steven Keats of *Seventh Avenue* as Jay Blackman
This New York-bred actor couldn't care less if his N.B.C. *Novel for Television* propels him into the superstar status. He's a serious actor with enough confidence and experience to get by.

(3) James Carroll Jordan of *Rich Man, Poor Man* (Billy)
(4) Gregg Henry of *Rich Man, Poor Man* (Wes)
(5) Meredith Baxter Birney of *Family* (Nancy)
(6) Gary Frank of *Family* (Willie)
(7) Mike Shera of *Barnaby Jones* (J.R.)
(8) Richard Hatch of *The Streets of San Francisco* (Dan Robbins)
(9) Shaun Cassidy of *The Hardy Boys* (Joe)
(10) Parker Stevenson of *The Hardy Boys* (Frank)
(11) Pamela Martin of *Nancy Drew* (Nancy)
(12) Mackenzie Phillips of *One Day at a Time* (Julie)
(13) Valeri Bertinelli of *One Day at a Time* (Barbara)
(14) Adam Arkin of *Busting Loose* (Lenny Markowitz)
(15) Vince Van Patten of *The Six Million Dollar Man* (The Bionic Boy)
(16) LaVar Burton of *Roots* (Kunta Kinte)
(17) George Sanford Brown of *Roots* (Tom)

THE GAME SHOWS

The Hollywood Squares
Peter Marshall was going nowhere. First as a singer, then as an actor, and finally as one-half a comedy team that made one service comedy during the fifties. But he hit his stride and kept it as the host of *The Hollywood Squares.*

Even though it's been on for more than ten years now, at first the producers needed three different pilots to convince them of its worth. It proved to be one of the most informative and funniest game shows in the history of television.

It combines personalities, quick wit, wealth, and information, all controlled by a giant tic-tac-toe board. The rules are simple, the winnings are ample, and a good time is guaranteed for all.

Many dozens of stars have come and gone in the nine "squares" over the years, but viewers also have a few regulars whom they can set their watches on. Rose Marie, the wisecracking co-writer on the original *Dick Van Dyke Show,* has found a permanent home in the top-middle square. Her jokes range from the frustration of spinsterhood to—well, the frustration of spinsterhood.

Charlie Weaver, or, as his friends knew him, Cliff Arquette, made his hilarious way in the lower-left-hand square for many years. His jokes were darts in the balloon of old age. His spryness and expansive good humor lit up the studio audience.

Recently, ol' lonesome George Gobel has occupied that space with his own brand of underdog humor. Jonathan Winters, Vincent Price, Karen Valentine, and, most recently, Waylon Flowers and Madame have given their careers much needed shots in the arm with exposure on the show.

And, of course, Paul Lynde. It would be safe to say that he was made on *The Hollywood Squares.* Even though he was getting by from his Broadway and Hollywood participation in *Bye, Bye Birdie,* Lynde was slowly sinking into second-rate obscurity when he took up residence in the center square on the N.B.C. game show. Since then he has risen to the very pinnacle of the comedy profession. He is known and loved all over the world, he is imitated incessantly, and his touring stage show almost unfailingly sells out.

Now Peter Marshall has his own variety show. Paul Lynde continues to get awards. There is talk of a record album of memorable questions and answers. And *Hollywood Squares* is awarded and loved internationally.

The Match Game
Back in the sixties Mark Goodson and Bill Todman, the creators of *The Price is Right* and *Concentration* among many others, had a new concept. It called for six contestants, three on each team, to try to match the answers of two

Gene Rayburn, host of "The Match Game".

celebrities, one the head of each team, in order to win prizes and money.

The show did moderately well, but viewer interest soon abated, and the program was cancelled. But Goodson and Todman still liked their conception and still thought it an eminently workable idea. So, years later they pulled the big switcheroo. Why not have two contestants try to match six celebrities instead of the other way around? They pulled out the old program, dusted it off, built a bright new set, and called back radio personality Gene Rayburn to host it.

The New Match Game was a huge surprise success, pulling in number-one ratings for the time period all over the country. Most of its reborn success was due to Gene and his regular panelists.

First, there was Brett Sommers, who was best known at the time as Jack Klugman's ex-wife. But on the show her rough humor and warm personality were displayed. Her characteristics were soon to become a dependable and running joke, as well as her pseudofeud with her "next-door regular" Charles Nelson Reilly.

Charles first came to prominence by starring as Cornelius to Carol Channing's matchmaker in *Hello, Dolly* on Broadway. Then television audiences got to know him as Hope Lange's real-estate agent and Edward Mulhare's foil on *The Ghost and Mrs. Muir*. His crazy demeanor and slightly fey manner were to become well known and greatly enjoyed on the game show.

Finally, Richard Dawson, an ex-nightclub comedian from London, who was first thrust into the limelight by *Hogan's Heroes,* in which he played the cockney card shark Newkirk. Following enthusiastically received visits on *The Merv Griffin Show* and others his dry wit was tapped for *The Match Game.*

There he's become known as a ladies' man and the best matcher on the show. Due to exposure (what he would be able to do with a line like that!) he has signed as the host of his own game show, *Family Feud.*

The Match Game continues to be strong in 1977, and the regulars have indeed become like a family. Gene Rayburn was also recently voted the sexiest game-show host by the readers of *Nighttime TV Magazine!*

Tattletales

Bert Convy was a Broadway actor as far back as 1959, when he was featured in the *Billy Barnes Revue.* He followed that up by starring in *Nowhere to Go But Up* in 1962 with a young actor named Tom Bosley (small-world time again). But in 1964 he got his big break. He had the leading role of Perchik in the original Broadway production of *Fiddler on the Roof* starring Zero Mostel (the role of Perchik was played in the movie version by Paul Michael Glaser—world's getting smaller all the time, ain't it?).

Bert followed his success by starring in *Cabaret* on Broadway two years later. And two years after that by leading the revival production of *The Front Page.*

But outside New York nobody knew him. He figured that, if he planned to continue much longer in the business, he had better get some other credits. So he traveled to California, where he made a Disney movie or two and costarred in *The Pigeon Sisters* with Helen Hayes, a doomed segment of the *N.B.C. Mystery Movie.*

Finally, Bert hit his stride as the host of *Tattletales,* another Goodson-Todman creation. There he developed a look (well-tailored suits with sweater vests) and a following. So now the whole country knows about Bert Convy.

The Gong Show

Chuck Barris was the maverick of the game-show world. He was one of the most original and outspoken producers of daytime entertainment. He was also one of the most heavily criticized. Many reporters felt that his programs were purposely demeaning and that his attitude was too self-serving and mercenary. But there was no doubt of his shows' successes.

The Dating Game was followed by *The Newlywed Game* only in taste. *The Dating Game,* hosted by Jim Lange, was structured around the concept that a person of one sex, usually a male, asked three other people of the opposite sex, usually female, inane questions so that he/she could choose the one he/she liked and the two of them could go on an all-expenses-paid date together (with a chaperone, of course).

The Newlywed Game, hosted by Bob Eubanks, had four newlywed couples humiliate each other for a prize hardly worth a cross word. On the show the couples were separated, and each partner asked leading questions about everything from their love life to whom they went with before they were married. Then the couples

The Cast of "Star Trek" on the bridge of the starship Enterprise.

were reunited, and each tried to guess the other's answer (a little like *Tattletales* but a lot more pathetic).

Thus began the love-hate relationship of Chuck Barris and the public. Barris followed up his winners with the relatively harmless *New Treasure Hunt* with Geoff Edwards but then took his love of the absurd and satire, combined them, and came up with *The Gong Show*.

The Gong Show was based on the old amateur talent shows of the forties. They are usually pictured in old Warner Brothers cartoons as an auditionee stopped by a bell, then dropped through a trap door or jerked offstage by a large shepherd's hook.

Chuck Barris took the concept and stretched it to a ridiculous length. Entertainment acts, ranging from the downright bizarre to the honestly talented, are rated by three guest-celebrity judges. If, after forty-five seconds, the act is considered so obscene or stupid or unwatchable or just plain bad that any of the judges wants it stopped, he has only to whack a giant gong hanging behind him with a large red mallet. The act with the highest score out of a possible thirty wins a gong award and a check for five hundred sixteen dollars and thirty-two cents (or seven hundred sixteen dollars and thirty-two cents, depending on whether it's the daytime or nighttime version of the show).

The nighttime version is hosted by the deep voice of Gary Owens, most commonly known as the on-screen announcer for the old *Rowan and Martin's Laugh-In*. The daytime show is hosted by none other than Chuck Barris himself!

Already the show and Barris' brand of laid-back master of absurdities have a following approaching legion proportions. *The Gong Show* has become a household word, and the concept, with Barris, set, and all, has been borrowed and featured on *The Carol Burnett Show* and *Sanford and Son*.

The weirder acts, such as a lady who burps to music, are usually never heard of again. But the stronger acts get a start and national exposure on the show. One singer was so good that he was immediately signed to do a segment of Burt Sugarman's *Midnight Special*.

CULT WORSHIP

Star Trek
What is this? It's been nine years since this

science-fiction program has gone off the air, but still the reruns are watched religiously, several dozen books by several authors under the label of two different publishers are selling briskly, annual conventions are held all over the country honoring the show and are attended by thousands, an entire generation of fans have been duly labeled with the nickname Trekkies, and now Paramount Studios is deep in the production of a multimillion-dollar *Star Trek* movie.

Well, I'm not going to analyze it. I am not even going to question it. It is too big for me. I am simply going to report the facts.

Star Trek appeared on the N.B.C. schedule on Thursdays during the 1966 season. It was the brainchild of an ex-policeman, now TV writer and producer named Gene Roddenberry. He was developing series conceptions for Desilu Productions (*Desi* Arnaz's and *Lu*cille Ball's company).

Gene had previously produced *The Lieutenant*, starring Gary Lockwood, and had written scripts for the likes of *Naked City, Have Gun, Will Travel,* and *Dr. Kildare*. His science fiction show had been two years in the making, with two different pilots, two different casts, and two different studios. Nevertheless, on September 8, 1966 the first episode of *Star Trek*, entitled "Man Trap" (this was the first to be seen by the public but the third made—due to last-minute panic on behalf of the network the original pilot, "Where No Man Has Gone Before," was shown two weeks later) was telecast.

The première story was about the Starship *Enterprise* checking up on a scientific colony on a distant planet in another galaxy. There they find that the only people left alive are a man and his "wife," who in reality is an alien vampire who can change her form at will and suck the salt out of human bodies. The intrepid crew of the *Enterprise* eliminates this threat and goes on to other adventures.

Although the program was to have a lasting effect on the millions of viewers who watched it, *Star Trek* did not immediately take off (if you'll excuse the expression). As a matter of fact, although it was of a quality rarely seen on television, let alone in science-fiction films, *Star Trek* had difficulty remaining in orbit for its first season. Either the ratings people weren't checking the right houses or they had some heavy competition. Whatever the reasons, *Star Trek* leveled off as a middle-of-the-road show.

The intrepid Captain, first officer, and engineer hold their own in the starship's engine room. From the left, Leonard Nimoy as Spock, William Shatner as Kirk and James Doohan as Scotty.

But too much money and time had been spent to simply pack in the show without a second chance, so *Star Trek* was renewed for another year. During the second season the show was shifted to Friday, the big dating night, which further wounded the faltering program. The quality remained high, but the show sank further in the Nielsens. Finally, N.B.C. saw no other recourse but to cancel the series.

That is when the phenomenal happened. Hundreds upon thousands of letters condemning the move swamped the N.B.C. offices. Daily demonstrations were held outside both the East and West Coast N.B.C. buildings, demanding *Star Trek*'s reinstatement.

The number of letters grew until the network workers could not handle them all. The number of demonstrators grew daily. Finally, N.B.C. succumbed to the pressure. *Star Trek* was renewed for a third season.

But a little too late, I'm afraid. The damage had been done. Because of the late word from N.B.C. Roddenberry and his staff had only approximately half the time that they normally would to produce the new episodes. It was a lot like a well-run machine that was left to run out of gas and grow cold. Starting it up again was a difficult process, involving a lot of stalling.

The last straw in *Star Trek's* initial demise was a time shift to 10:00 P.M. Friday night. Now not only would the young dating adults miss it but the preteen audience, who had to go to bed early, as well. The series' production and writing values sunk as the rating did. At midseason *Star Trek* was left to drift to the rerun syndicators and given its last rites by N.B.C.

The show wouldn't die. Fans everywhere stayed loyal to it, and in human terms the show took on martyr standing. Its fame grew and spread until no one could ignore it.

Daily reruns remain high in the ratings. Dramatizations of the screenplays were written for Bantam Books by the late James Blish. A Saturday-morning cartoon show was made. Dramatizations of the cartoon scripts were written by the rising science fiction author Alan Dean Foster for Ballantine Books. A line of *Star Trek* clothing was created. Plastic models of the *Enterprise,* shuttle craft, Klingon warship, bridge, Romulan cruiser, and Mr. Spock are all-time bestsellers. Several major businesses were

formed and are prospering just by handling the fan reaction. *Star Trek* dolls, lunchboxes, weapons, and communicators sell briskly. *The Star Trek Technical Manual* made the bestseller lists at six dollars and ninety-five cents a shot.

And finally, Gene Roddenberry is producing the *Star Trek* movie for Paramount. Alan Scott and Chris Bryant, authors of one of the best horror movies ever made, *Don't Look Now,* are writing the script, and Phil Kaufman, whose only other credit is *The White Dawn,* an Antarctic survival movie, will direct the *Star Trek* feature, which is due for a late 1977 or early 1978 release.

Following that movie Roddenberry hopes to use the already built sets for an all-new *Star Trek* television series. It seems as if the era of *Star Trek* is only beginning!

The Muppet Show
A brand new kind of hero worship has started. In the past great men and women were worshipped. Now, because of the fertile mind of a man named Jim Henson, a small green frog is being worshipped. A frog named Kermit.

Kermit is the undisputed leader of a crew of crazy puppets named, for identity's sake, the Muppets. Their brand of humor and visual personality are unique, and their fame has grown from variety shows to children's shows to a show of their own until viewing has become a family affair.

The first Muppet to gain national attention was Ralph the Dog (now seen as the piano player and Dr. Bob on the show), who appeared on the old *Jimmy Dean Show.* While that was going strong, Jim Henson, the creator and brain behind them (or under them, as it were), whipped humorous skits up for a variety of unique hand puppets to partake in. The wit and style of these bits were displayed on the *Ed Sullivan Show* among others. The Muppets' brand of fun pleased all ages and was soon almost immediately recognizable.

The real break came with the advent of *Sesame Street,* the revolutionary children's show on the Public Broadcasting System. It marked a whole new way of using TV in education. It also presented the Muppets in a new and delightful form. Soon each of the Muppets had his own individual identity and name. Besides Ralph and Kermit there was Oscar the Grouch.

Michelle Nichols as Lt. Uhura, communications officer.

the Cookie Monster, Ernie and Bert, Grover, various and sundry people, slugs, aliens, and monsters, as well as a seven-foot-tall, yellow-feathered walking Muppet named Big Bird.

Finally, Henson and his by then huge crew couldn't be contained. There were Muppet records and a whole line of toys. The Muppets branched out to be semiregulars on *N.B.C.'s Saturday Night,* and then, on the strength of a half-hour special, Henson and the folks made a deal with C.B.S. to produce a weekly variety show.

Right away most of the syndicated programs were rated number one in their time zones. A whole new set of intricate, complicated, and fascinating Muppets was introduced. Fozzie, the teddy-bear comedian; Scooter, the backstage gopher; Waldorf and Sheraton, the two elderly hecklers; Animal, the maniacal drummer, Dr. Teeth and the Electric Mayhem, a rock group; and various eight-foot monsters, talking French breads, anarchists, and animals. Anything can and usually does happen on *The Muppet Show.*

Saturday Night Live

N.B.C. took a dare. Their Saturday late-night spot was empty. For years they had been filling it with reruns of *The Tonight Show* and an occasional segment of *Weekend,* their newsmagazine show.

Well, in a moment of insanity by all practical standards, they decided to let a new young producer named Lorne Michaels have his way. Michaels suggested that they leave the time from 11:30 P.M. to 1:00 A.M. open for live music and satire, reminiscent of the fifties' comedy *Your Show of Shows* but with a hearty dose of *Monty Python.*

N.B.C. said, why not? They thought that they had nothing to lose, so they gave the time period to Michaels. Michaels went crazy. And not the way Penny Marshall went crazy when she discovered that the rest of the world wasn't Jewish. No, Lorne went crazy like a fox.

He put together a team of young, avant-garde comedy writers, collected a versatile group of actors, lined up an impressive list of guest stars in every area of the entertainment field, put them all together, shook briskly, and got *N.B.C.'s Saturday Night!* The biggest thing since hula hoops.

Their brand of tradition-breaking, censor-ship-begging, morality-teasing satire has caught on and held. Satire including commercials for speed, a series of episodes called Samurai Tailor, Samurai Divorce Court, etc.; the Weekend Update segment (I'm Chevy Chase, and you're not), and the Claudine Longet Invitational Ski Meet and Skeet Shoot.

More unusual than *The Gong Show!* Dirtier than Dean Martin! Able to leap pretension in a single bound! Look, high in the ratings, it's a lemon, it's a bomb, no! It's Saaaaaturday NIGHT!!!

The acting crew, affectionately termed The Not Ready For Prime Time Players, was made up of Dan Ackroyd, the fastest voice in the biz; John Belushi, of the off-Broadway *National Lampoon* show, *Lemmings,* where he first presented his Joe Cocker impersonation; Chevy Chase, who was picked from the writing staff to perform and was also in *Lemmings* as John Denver; Jane Curtain; Garrett Morris from *Car Wash;* Gilda Radner; and Lorraine Newman.

Chase has gone on to a new contract with N.B.C. for specials, while the rest happily remain Not Ready For Prime Time Players.

Mary Hartman, Mary Hartman

Norman Lear was responsible for everything but violence. That goes back a long way on television, but, if you want to complain about profanity, controversial issues, sex, and loose morality on television anywhere other than in the news, just write Norman Lear. It's his fault.

He originally broke the mold with *All in the Family* in 1971. It described the hilarious adventures of a WASP dyed-in-the-wool bigot and his family. Lear created the concept after producing a variety of funny but mostly failed films, including *Cold Turkey* with Dick Van Dyke and *Start the Revolution Without Me,* starring Gene Wilder and Donald Sutherland. *All in the Family* was based on an English BBC comedy called *'Till Death Do Us Part* and is more or less the same idea but with the name changed to Bunker.

Well, Archie's battle with the Meathead was an instantaneous (what's another word for success? All through this book it seems that I've used that word hundreds of times. I need some variation. Let's see, now. Smash? No, used it. Hit? Nope. Smash hit? It's beginning to sound like the sound effects for a mugging. Ah, I know.

Spock and Kirk look forward to more missions thanks to the new "Star Trek".

The old way comics were done on TV. It wasn't any "Wonder Woman".
Batman, first season.

Louise Lasser as Mary Hartman.

winner—well, at least it's different). Lear followed that up with *Sanford and Son*, which was based on another English show, *Steptoe and Son*. Then it was spinoff time! *Maude, Good Times*, and *The Jeffersons* followed in rapid succession. Then came *All's Fair, One Day at a Time*, and the *Hot L Baltimore*. Some winners, some losers.

But after awhile show piled on show, concept piled on concept. Nothing seemed new and original anymore. Until Lear reached into his files and dusted off an old idea for a soap-opera satire. Now *that* had possibilities.

Seven years before Lear had first approached A.B.C. They were itching for a hit series, so Norman set up a deal for them to produce some experimental episodes. But they soon got cold feet and backed out of the deal.

Fred Silverman, then with the number-one-ranked C.B.S., got involved and put money down to finance some sample scripts. When he saw them, however, he passed judgment. Too weird to sell, he decreed, so Lear went to N.B.C. But they agreed with Silverman.

The more the major networks came down on the idea, the better it sounded to Norman. When he began to feel stale years later, he saw it as another chance for a major media breakthrough. So he went ahead and hired top comedy writers, including Ann Marcus, contributor to *National Lampoon* and *Saturday Night Live* as well as editor for the feminist humor book *Titters,* and Gail Parent, author of *Sheila Levine is Dead and Living in New York* and *David Meyer is a Mother* (no relation).

After the pilot was produced, Lear invited the syndicated stations to come and have a look. They liked what they saw, and soon *Mary Hartman, Mary Hartman* began to sell. And as soon as it was seen, a wave of controversy began. First as a minor squall, then as a major hurricane.

With a plot line like MH2's, most people's complaints were justified. The American public had never seen anything like this before on TV. In the first season alone Mary Hartman's grandfather was arrested for indecent exposure; her sister was engaged to a deaf-mute and then to a priest; her neighbor drowned in a bowl of her chicken soup; her other neighbor was paralyzed from a car accident with five nuns; her husband

had an affair and became an alcoholic; and she herself was held hostage by a mass murderer, then had a nervous breakdown on *The David Susskind Show*.

And all the preceding was dished up with a combination of soap-opera clichés and inspired insanity. The MH2 enthusiasts soon outnumbered the nay-sayers. Watching MH2 became the in thing to do. Newspapers began running synopses of the previous day's plots to keep the readership up to date. For its first season MH2 was an unqualified (ummmm, let's see, now) triumph (or success, what have you).

Still, it was losing money. The price of production exceeded the price that the syndicated stations were paying. So, during the summer hiatus Norman Lear acquired even more syndicated stations and renegotiated a higher per-episode price.

But something strange (abnormal, odd, weird, queer, funny, bewildering, startling—take your pick) happened in its second season. The plot lines were still a bizarre mishmash, but people were biginning to turn off Mary's manic misadventures. The quality of the writing began to dip, and lengthy articles concerning the drop in style began to appear. Norman Lear was forced to make some fast changes and harsh speeches.

It seemed that the entire atmosphere on the MH2 set had been steadily deteriorating. Louise Lasser, Woody Allen's ex-wife and star of the show, had been described as impossible and a kvetch as well as being arrested for possession of illegal drugs (cocaine). Bruce Soloman, who played the first season's heart throb, Sgt. Dennis Foley, had asked for too many concessions in his new contract and had to be released (he is now playing Rabbi David Small opposite Art Carney in the N.B.C. series *Lanigan's Rabbi*). The writing staff had become more and more lackadaisical. That is, until Norman put his foot down. And these days his foot carries a lot of weight. He made it clear that no one but no one was unexpendable.

Suddenly, bold new plot devices began appearing; the acting crew began to work together again; new characters were introduced. From all outward signs *Mary Hartman, Mary Hartman* is back on the right track.